EMMANUEL
The Man Who Is God
Volume Two

Studies in Christology

Dr. Ken Chant

EMMANUEL

The Man Who Is God

Volume Two

Studies in Christology

By Ken Chant

Copyright © 2013 Ken Chant

ISBN 978-1-61529-093-2

Vision Publishing
1672 Main Street E 109
Ramona, CA 92065
1 800-9-VISION
WWW.BOOKSBYVISION.COM

All rights reserved worldwide. No part of this book may be reproduced in any manner without the written permission of the author except in brief quotations embodied in critical articles or reviews.

A NOTE ON GENDER

It is unfortunate that the English language does not contain an adequate generic pronoun (especially in the singular number) that includes without bias both male and female. So "he, him, his, man, mankind," with their plurals, must do the work for both sexes. Accordingly, wherever it is appropriate to do so in the following pages, please include the feminine gender in the masculine, and vice versa.

FOOTNOTES

A work once fully referenced will thereafter be noted either by "ibid" or "op. cit."

Contents

AN EASTER HYMN 5
SMOKY GLASS 7
JESUS HARROWING HELL 9
CHAPTER ONE THE MAN WHO IS GOD 13
CHAPTER TWO THE ETERNAL LOGOS 19
CHAPTER THREE THE WITNESS OF HIS MIRACLES 39
CHAPTER FOUR THE WITNESS OF THE FATHERS 45
CHAPTER FIVE EXTRAORDINARY BENEFITS 53
CHAPTER SIX CREEDS AND CANONS 63
CHAPTER SEVEN A CLUSTER OF HERESIES 71
CHAPTER EIGHT EVER WITH THE FATHER 91
CHAPTER NINE CHRIST AND CREATION 105
CHAPTER TEN BORN OF A WOMAN 115
CHAPTER ELEVEN PERSEUS AND ASCLEPIUS 123
CHAPTER TWELVE OVERSHADOWED BY THE SPIRIT 135
CHAPTER THIRTEEN ABASED AND EXALTED 143
CHAPTER FOURTEEN A MAGNIFICENT HYMN 151
CHAPTER FIFTEEN THE FORM OF A SERVANT 161
CHAPTER SIXTEEN THE MAN OF CALVARY 181
CHAPTER SEVENTEEN THE GOSPEL AND THE WORLD 193
CHAPTER EIGHTEEN THE FULNESS OF CHRIST 201
CHAPTER NINETEEN LIFE IN CHRIST 213
ADDENDUM THE CATHOLIC VIEW 221

ABBREVIATIONS

Abbreviations commonly used for the books of the Bible are

Genesis	Ge	Habakkuk	Hb
Exodus	Ex	Zephaniah	Zp
Leviticus	Le	Haggai	Hg
Numbers	Nu	Zechariah	Zc
Deuteronomy	De	Malachi	Mal
Joshua	Js		
Judges	Jg		
Ruth	Ru	Matthew	Mt
1 Samuel	1 Sa	Mark	Mk
2 Samuel	2 Sa	Luke	Lu
1 Kings	1 Kg	John	Jn
2 Kings	2 Kg	Acts	Ac
1 Chronicles	1 Ch	Romans	Ro
2 Chronicles	2 Ch	1 Corinthians	1 Co
Ezra	Ezr	2 Corinthians	2 Co
Nehemiah	Ne	Galatians	Ga
Esther	Es	Ephesians	Ep
Job	Jb	Philippians	Ph
Psalm	Ps	Colossians	Cl
Proverbs	Pr	1 Thessalonians	1 Th
Ecclesiastes	Ec	2 Thessalonians	2 Th
Song of Songs	Ca *	1 Timothy	1 Ti
Isaiah	Is	2 Timothy	2 Ti
Jeremiah	Je	Titus	Tit
Lamentations	La	Philemon	Phm
Ezekiel	Ez	Hebrews	He
Daniel	Da	James	Ja
Hosea	Ho	1 Peter	1 Pe
Joel	Jl	2 Peter	2 Pe
Amos	Am	1 John	1 Jn
Obadiah	Ob	2 John	2 Jn
Jonah	Jo	3 John	3 Jn
Micah	Mi	Jude	Ju
Nahum	Na	Revelation	Re

Ca is an abbreviation of *Canticles,* a derivative of the Latin name of the *Song of Solomon,* which is sometimes also called the *Song of Songs.*

Note: scripture translations are my own unless otherwise noted.

An Easter Hymn

Most glorious Lord of life, that on this day,
Didst make thy triumph over death and sin –
And having **harrow'd hell**, didst bring away
Captivity thence captive, us to win –
This joyous day, dear Lord, with joy begin,
And grant that we for whom thou diddest die,
Being with thy dear blood clean wash'd from sin,
May live for ever in felicity.
And that thy love we weighing worthily,
May likewise love thee for the same again –
And for thy sake, that all like dear didst buy,
With love may one another entertain.
So let us love, dear love, like as we ought,
Love is the lesson which the Lord us taught. [1]

---

(1)   Edmund Spenser (1552?-1599). The poem was first published in 1595 as one of eighty-eight sonnets. It was probably written between 1592 and 1594 during the poet's wooing of Elizabeth Boyle. "This day" refers to Easter Sunday. The "harrowing of hell" (the emphasis above is mine) refers to the descent of Christ into Hades, where, according to an ancient Christian myth, he succoured the souls of the just and carried them away from that bleak place. The story is charmingly related in the apocryphal Gospel of Nicodemus – Part Two. (See the selection just below.)

Smoky Glass

John Oxenham, an early 20th century British Christian novelist and poet, was frequently approached by aspiring authors who hoped that he would share with them some magic key to successful writing. He always insisted that no one should ever take up a pen unless they were driven by an irresistible compulsion to write, and that their theme should be burning in their souls. Without this, said he, their outpourings would lie dull and sickly on the page. He responded to one enquirer with this quatrain –

> Write if you must,
> But – think on this –
> Christ wrote but once
> And then in dust.

Well, I can say truthfully enough that I felt compelled to write this book, along with its companion (*Emmanuel – Part One*). And I hope it will not be so ephemeral as the words Jesus wrote with his finger in the dirt! Not that I pretend to have said anything truly new, for after 20 centuries, who could hope to do that? But I may have said at least *some* things in a new way, or approached them from a different direction.

And now both books are done.

Am I satisfied? No. For the theme is too enormous, too high, too deep, too wide, for any human mind or speech to embrace wholly. But I can at least look the Lord in the eye and say that I have done my best.

Do I know more than when I began? That too is doubtful! Here I am (2013) – after 60 years of ministry as a pastor, teacher, preacher, writer – feeling obliged to echo the sad words of Omar Khayyam (*c.* 1048-*c.* 1122), Persian poet, mathematician, and astronomer, who wrote the following epitaph on his life of scholarship – (2)

> My mind has never lacked learning;
> Few mysteries remain unconned;
> I have meditated for 72 years night and day,
> To learn that nothing has been learned at all!

But mayhap that is too pessimistic. One does, of course, learn *something*. But one also learns that all knowledge is fraught with uncertainty, that nothing is ever fully known. As Paul said, even the very smartest among us are little better than people looking though a piece of smoky glass, with an occasional clear patch. We see only in part, we know only in part, and this side of the resurrection we cannot hope for better (1 Co 13:9,12).

So I have written two books about Jesus, *Son of Man* and *Son of God*. But in the end I must confess that I know nothing! What is a candle when set against the sun? What is a grain of dust beside a mountain, a drop of water flung up by the vast ocean? Indeed, who among us has anything of which to boast. Whatever we have that is useful was given to us by the Father; for the rest, it is but dust. So, like all others, these two books of mine will eventually perish and be forgotten, their value long since exhausted. But one volume will remain – *God's Book* – which will endure even beyond the dissolution of heaven and earth and all that is in them.

---

(2) <u>The Ruba'iyat of Omar Khayyam</u>, tr. by Peter Avery and John-Heath-Stubbs; Penguin Classics, 1983; *Quatrain 191*.

Jesus Harrowing Hell

(from the 2nd cent. apocryphal *Gospel of Nicodemus*)

Satan the heir of darkness, (3) came and said to Hades – O all-devouring and insatiable, hear my words. There is of the race of the Jews one named Jesus, calling himself the Son of God; and being a man, by our working with them the Jews have crucified him – and now when he is dead, be ready that we may secure him here. For I know that he is a man ... (yet) he has also done me many evils when living with mortals in the upper world. For wherever he found my servants, he persecuted them; and whatever men I made crooked, blind, lame, lepers, or any such thing, by a single word he healed them; and many whom I had got ready to be buried, even these through a single word he brought to life again.

Hades says – And is this man so powerful as to do such things by a single word? or if he be so, canst thou withstand him? It seems to me that, if he be so, no one will be able to withstand him. ... Satan says – O all-devouring and insatiable Hades, art thou so afraid at hearing of our common enemy? I was not afraid of him, but worked in the Jews, and they crucified him, and gave him also to drink gall with vinegar. Make ready, then, in order that you may lay fast hold of him when he comes.

Hades answered – Heir of darkness, son of destruction, devil, thou hast just now told me that many whom thou hadst made ready to be buried, he brought to life again by a

---

(3)   See footnote (1). The selection above comes from chapters 4-8. See <u>The Ante-Nicene Fathers</u>; Eerdmans Publishing Company, Grand Rapids, Michigan; 1978 reprint; Vol. 8, pg. 436-438; hereinafter referred to as ANF.

single word. And if he has delivered others from the tomb, how and with what power shall he be laid hold of by us? For I not long ago swallowed down one dead, Lazarus by name; and not long after, one of the living by a single word dragged him up by force out of my bowels – and I think that it was he of whom thou speakest. If, therefore, we receive him here, I am afraid lest perchance we be in danger even about the rest. ... Wherefore also I adjure even thee, for thy benefit and for mine, not to bring him here; for I think that he is coming here to raise all the dead. And this I tell thee – by the darkness in which we live, if thou bring him here, not one of the dead will be left behind in it to me.

While Satan and Hades were thus speaking to each other, there was a great voice like thunder, saying – Lift up your gates, O ye rulers; and be ye lifted up, ye everlasting gates; and the King of glory shall come in. When Hades heard, he said to Satan – Go forth, if thou art able, and withstand him. Satan therefore went forth to the outside. Then Hades says to his demons – Secure well and strongly the gates of brass and the bars of iron, and attend to my bolts, and stand in order, and see to everything; for if he come in here, woe will seize us. ...

And immediately with these words the brazen gates were shattered, and the iron bars broken, and all the dead who had been bound came out of the prisons ... And the King of glory came in, in the form of a man, and all the dark places of Hades were lighted up. Immediately Hades cried out – We have been conquered – woe to us! But who art thou, that hast such power and might? and what art thou, who comest here without sin who art seen to be small and yet of great power, lowly and exalted, the slave and the master, the soldier and the king, who hast power over the dead and the living? Thou wast nailed on the cross, and placed in the tomb; and now thou art free, and hast destroyed all our power. Art thou then the Jesus about whom the chief satrap Satan told us, that through cross and death thou art to inherit the whole world?

Then the King of glory seized the chief satrap Satan by the head, and delivered him to his angels, and said – With iron chains bind his hands and his feet, and his neck, and his mouth. Then he delivered him to Hades, and said – Take him, and keep him secure till my second appearing.

And Hades receiving Satan, said to him – Beelzebul, heir of fire and punishment, enemy of the saints, through what necessity didst thou bring about that the King of glory should be crucified, so that he should come here and deprive us of our power? Turn and see that not one of the dead has been left in me, but all that thou hast gained through the tree of knowledge, all hast thou lost through the tree of the cross – and all thy joy has been turned into grief; and wishing to put to death the King of glory, thou hast put thyself to death. For, since I have received thee to keep thee safe, by experience shall thou learn how many evils I shall do unto thee. O arch-devil, the beginning of death, root of sin, end of all evil, what evil didst thou find in Jesus, that thou shouldst compass his destruction? how hast thou dared to do such evil? how hast thou busied thyself to bring down such a man into this darkness, through whom thou hast been deprived of all who have died from eternity?

While Hades was thus discoursing to Satan, the King of glory stretched out his right hand, and took hold of ... all the prophets and the saints (who) said – We thank Thee, O Christ, Saviour of the world, that Thou hast brought our life up out of destruction.

And after they had thus spoken, the Saviour ... took them, and sprang up out of Hades. And while he was going, the holy fathers accompanying him sang praises, saying – Blessed is he that cometh in the name of the Lord – Alleluia; to him be the glory of all the saints.

Chapter One

THE MAN WHO IS GOD

How great is this mystery, that God has dwelt among us in the flesh! Were we to ponder it across the eternal ages we still would not comprehend its wonder. Yet amazement and joy increase for ever as we grow in understanding and faith. In this second of two volumes we continue our quest for the true identity of Christ, *Son of Man* and *Son of God*. Having explored in *Part One* the witness given both by the prophets and by Christ himself about his deity, we will now consider ...

THE WITNESS OF THE APOSTLES

It is hard to know where to start! The evidence is written on almost every page of the NT. Sometimes consciously, sometimes unconsciously, the apostles continually exalt Christ to the pinnacle of heaven. They could not refrain from giving him the highest possible honour.

My original intention was to provide an exhaustive list of NT references to the deity of Christ. But I soon realised that such a discussion would be not only exhaust*ive*, but exhaust*ing*! Instead, I will concentrate on a few of the more striking references, and hope you will find the proof sufficiently fascinating and convincing.

PRAYER IS OFFERED TO CHRIST

The NT not only teaches that prayer should be offered to the Father in the name of Jesus, but that Christ too can be addressed in prayer –

- 2 Corinthians 13:14 – "The grace of the Lord Jesus Christ and the love of God and the fellowship of the Holy Spirit be with you all."

That is a simple prayer – to **Christ** for grace, to **God** for love, and to the **Spirit** for fellowship. It involves the entire Godhead, for three prayers are spoken, one each to the Son, the Father, and the Holy Spirit. The prayer pre-supposes that each of those Persons is fully able to hear and answer it, no matter when it is offered, or by whom.

Notice also how Paul's benediction presupposes also *equality* of the Son with the Father, and of the Spirit with the Son – for if they were not equal it would be verging on blasphemy to link their names so familiarly. Further, see how Paul refers to Christ first, the Spirit last, and places the Father in the middle. Could he have done that unless he felt it was proper to give Christ the honour that belongs to God?

Can you imagine, for instance, Paul writing – *"May the assistance of Michael the archangel, and the grace of Jesus the Son, and the love of God the Father, be given to you"*? He would not have dared to associate even an archangel's name so closely with either Christ or the Father – because such a link, within a prayerful benediction, does infer equality of honour and power among each of the persons addressed.[4]

---

(4)   2 Co 13:14 is one of the NT references that support the idea of the "Trinity" – that is, the doctrine that within the one God there are three who are equal in essence, nature, and power, while differing in person and office. The word "Trinity" does not occur in scripture. It was coined by theologians to describe their effort to unify all that the Bible tells us about the Father, the Son, and the Holy Spirit. Despite 20 centuries of thought and prayer, even the best formulations of trinitarian doctrine remain an inadequate description of the Godhead – probably because no human words can ever sufficiently define an infinite Deity. The need for such a doctrine arises from two simple facts: *(i)* the Bible declares
(continued on next page)

- **1 Thessalonians 3:11; 2 Th 2:16** – "Now may our God and Father himself, and our Lord Jesus, direct our way to you ... Now may our Lord Jesus Christ himself, and God our Father ... comfort your hearts."

The similarity in the form of those two prayers is obvious, except that in one *"the Father himself"* is addressed first, and in the other *"Jesus himself"* is addressed first. It is difficult to see how Paul could have composed such benedictions, unless in his mind there was no difference in the honour that belongs both to Christ and to the Father.

- **John 14:13,14; Jn 16:23** – "Whatever you ask in my name I will do it ... if you ask anything in my name I will do it ... If you ask anything of the Father, he will give it to you in my name."

First, Jesus says that we can pray directly to *him*, and he will himself answer the prayer; but then, second, we ask the *Father* in Jesus' name, and the Father will answer. This is strange talk, unless Jesus has the same ability to answer prayer as the Father – which means he must have the properties of deity, for who can answer prayer but God?

- ***John 5:13-15*** – The Son of God, says John, hears us when we pray, and promises to give us whatever we ask, so long as we pray in faith, and in harmony with his will. Other references to Christ being addressed in prayer are *Acts 7:59-60; 22:19-20; 1 Corinthians 1:2*.

Now, as I have just said, only God has the attributes necessary to hear and to answer the prayers of people in

---

(continued from previous page)

unequivocally that God is one (De 6:4); *(ii)* yet the same Bible just as clearly ascribes divine attributes to three persons, the Father, the Son, and the Holy Spirit. Trinitarian doctrine is a noble attempt to reconcile those seemingly disparate propositions; that is, to show that God is truly Three in One.

every nation; anyone who says he can hear and answer prayer, wherever and whenever it is offered, is plainly asserting that he is God. Jesus made that assertion of himself, and the apostles firmly endorsed it. What else can this mean except that *Christ is God*?

CHRIST HAS THE ATTRIBUTES OF GOD

Here is a list of the divine attributes scripture gives to Christ. It is an expanded version of a list first prepared by A. S. Martin –

- he has self-existence, like the Father (Jn 5:26)
- his life is eternal, without beginning or end (Jn 1:4; 1:25; 14:6; 17:5)
- he has pre-existence (He 7:3; Re 1:8)
- he cannot yield to death, nor see corruption (Jn 10:18; Ro 1:4; He 7:16; Jn 11:25; Ac 13:37; 2:27).
- he gives the Holy Spirit (Ac 2:33-36)
- he will come again (Jn 14:3,28; Ac 1:11; 1 Co 11:26; etc.)
- he gives life to others (Jn 5:25,21; 6:40; Ph 3:10,11)
- he possesses absolute holiness (Lu 1:35; Jn 6:69; He 7:26)
- he is immutable, as changeless as Yahweh (cp. Ps 102:12 with He 1:11,12; 13:8)
- he is omnipotent (Mt 18:18; Re 1:8; Jn 5:19; He 1:3; Ph 2:9; and he is able to communicate this power to his disciples: Ac 9:34; 3:16; 4:10)
- he is omniscient (Ac 1:24; 1 Co 4:5; Cl 2:3)

- he is omnipresent (Mt 28:20; Ep 1:23)
- the Divine Plenitude dwells in him (Cl 2:9) [5]

All those attributes are the rightful properties only of *deity*. Whoever possesses them must be God, for only God *can* possess them.

CHRIST PERFORMS THE WORKS OF GOD

Three classes of works are ascribed to Christ in the NT – those which any human being can do; those which can be done through communicated power (such as miracles of healing done by the power of the Holy Spirit); and those which only unaided deity can perform. Martin gives the following list of places where this third class of works is ascribed to Christ –

- *Creation* (Jn 1:3; Cl 1:16,17; He 1:2,10)
- *Providence* (He 1:3; Jn 5:17; Cl 1:17)
- *Redemption* (Ac 20:28; Jn 13:18,10,16; Mt 9:13; Ep 5:26; passages too numerous to be specified)
- *Forgiveness* (Mt 9:6; Mk 2:10; Lu 5:24; etc.)
- *Judgment* (Jn 5:22, 27; Ac 17:31; Ro 14:10; Mt 25:31-46)
- *Restoration* (Ph 3:21; 1 Co 15:24-28).

    Finally the whole atmosphere of feeling and disposition towards Christ in the NT is one of worship. He claims it, and his disciples accord it. The faith given to God is given to him (Jn

---

(5) Dictionary of the New Testament, Vol. I, "Christ and the Gospels;" edited by James Hastings; reprinted by Baker Book House, Grand Rapids, Michigan, 1973; pg. 479.

> *14:1; etc.). Examples of doxologies are – 1 Pe 4:11; 2 Ti 4:18; Re 1:6; 2 Pe 3:18; Re 5:13. The honour of the Son equals that of the Father (Jn 5:23; Ph 2:9,10; He 1:6).* (6)

If God alone can do such things, and if it is true that Christ does them, then Christ must be God.

---

(6)   Ibid.

Chapter Two

THE ETERNAL LOGOS

If we could find only one place in the NT where Christ is specifically called God, then that should end all argument about his deity. There are indeed a number of places where Christ appears to be called "God", yet because of the peculiarities of the Greek language, or because of an uncertain textual authority, each of the references has been contested. You will have to form your own opinion –

TEXTS THAT ARE PROBABLY SPURIOUS

There are three texts that were once popular proofs of the deity of Christ, but they are hardly ever used now. Better knowledge of the Greek language and of the early NT manuscripts has caused these texts to be revised –

- **_Acts 20:28_**, used to read – *"Feed the church of God, which he has purchased with his own blood."* That reading implies that it was God himself who died on the cross – therefore, Christ is God.

It is still uncertain precisely what Luke wrote, but most exegetes are agreed that it was probably – *"Feed the church of the Lord"* (as in the RSV); or, *"Feed the church of God, which he has purchased with the blood of his Son"* (not, *"with his own blood"*).

- **_1 Timothy 3:16_**, used to read, *"God was manifest in the flesh,"* but should probably read, *"Who was manifest in the flesh"* (as in the RSV footnote, Alford's Greek Testament, Zerwick and Grosvenor, and many others).

- **_1 John 5:7_**, used to include the words, "There are three that bear record in heaven, the Father, the

Word, and the Holy Spirit, and these three are one." According to Alford, those words are omitted from all Greek MSS previous to the beginning of the 16th century; all the Greek Fathers (even when producing texts in support of the doctrine of the Holy Trinity ...); all the ancient versions ...; and many Latin Fathers. [7]

The conclusion is that those words were never part of John's original letter, but were added to the letter by a later hand.

However, the cause is not lost! There *are* passages that either state or imply the full deity of Christ –

TEXTS THAT CALL CHRIST GOD

- **John 1:1**, "In the beginning was the Word, and the Word was with God, and the Word was God."

Since everyone agrees that *"The Word"* is another name for Christ, this verse appears to say clearly that Christ is God.

THE ARIAN VIEW

Arians [8] try to avoid the above conclusion, by arguing that the Greek text can be and should be translated thus – *"The Word was with God, and the Word was divine"* (that is, "a god").

They claim that the Greek word for "god" (theos) is linked with a definite article in the first place, but not in the second. [9] In Greek it looks like this –

kai ho logos een pros ton theon, kai theos een ho logos

---

(7) Henry Alford, Greek Testament, Vol. 4, Guardian Press, Grand Rapids, Michigan; 1976 reprint; pg. 503.

(8) You will find an explanation of *Arianism* in Chapter Seven below.

(9) If your grammar is rusty, "the definite article" is simply the word "the". In Greek, it is "ho".

and the word was with (the) god and god was the word

It is argued that the existence of the definite article in front of *logos*, and in front of the first *theos*, shows that those words should be translated as "Word" and "God" (both with initial capitals) – referring to Christ and to the true God. Nobody quarrels with that. But Arians then go on to say, conversely, that the *absence* of the definite article from the second *theos* shows that the reference there is not to the true God, but to a "god" – which is a way of saying that while Christ is divine, he is less than God.

Is that a valid argument?

"DIVINITY" OR "DEITY"?

In the clause, *"and god was the word,"* the subject in Greek is not "god" (*theos*), but "the word" (*ho logos*). *Theos* in this clause is called the predicate – that is, it is placed in the sentence to express something about the subject. That is the grammatical significance (in Greek) of omitting the definite article from *theos*, but including it with *logos*. The presence of the article shows that *logos* is the subject, and its omission shows that *theos* is the predicate. That is why the English translators change the order of the words, so that they read, "and the *logos* was *theos*." We prefer to put the subject first and the predicate second.

Now we have already seen that *ho logos* should be translated, "the Word;" but what about *theos* (without the definite article)? Should this be read as "a god," "God," or "divine"? If "divine" is taken to mean something less than God, then that translation cannot be allowed, for the Greeks had another word to express this – *theios*, which in Greek had about the same relationship to *theos* as in English "divinity" sometimes has to "deity." Having already used *theos* to refer to the true God in the clause, *"the Word was with God,"* it is improbable that John would use *theos* in a lesser sense in the next clause – especially when the other word (*theios*) was available if he had really wanted to say that the Word was *divine,* but not *God.*

A SUBTLE EMPHASIS

That his second *theos* should be translated "God" is shown by the order in which John has placed his words. He could have followed the natural order –

subject	verb	predicate
the Word	was	God

Instead, John uses the order –

predicate	verb	subject
God	was	the Word

That inverted word order has the effect, in Greek, of placing special emphasis on *theos*. It is in fact a way of preventing any attempt to make this *theos* mean anything less than the previous one. It shows that John was referring, not to "a god," but to "God." In other words, the Arians are wrong, for the Greek construction requires that *theos* be given the same meaning in each place. John has built his sentence in a way that forbids following a strong translation of the first occurrence by a weak translation of the second.

A FINE DISTINCTION

The use of an inversion, and the use of the definite article, are ways in Greek (as they may also be in English) of achieving emphasis. Thus, in the following example, the first statement is stronger than the second –

"Few are the followers of Christ." – "There are few followers of Christ."

Notice **(a)** the inversion of the predicate (*few*) and **(b)** the use of the definite article (*the*) in the first example. Using those two devices has the effect of giving the first sentence greater vigour.

But why does John use *both* of those forms in one short sentence? Why does he not simply use *ho theos* (= God) in both places? Surely it would have been simpler and better for him to have followed a more common construction? Perhaps like this –

kai ho logos	een pros	ton theon	kai ho logos	een	ho theos ⁽¹⁰⁾
and the Word	was with	the God	and the Word	was	the God

At first sight, that amended construction would seem to solve all the problems, by making an unequivocal statement of the full deity of Christ. Why then didn't John use it? There are two very important reasons why John could not possibly have written

kai ho logos een ho theos
and the Word was (the) God.

They are –

FIRST – THE SAME – YET DIFFERENT!

Having just said, in the previous clause, *"the Word was with God,"* it would then be nonsense to say, without any qualification, *"the Word was God."* That, of course, is the problem with our English translation (*"the Word was with God, and the Word was God."*) As it stands, it is

---

(10)   This construction is often used. For example, 1 Co 10:4 –

- *he petra een ho Christos* – "the Rock was (the) Christ"

- So if grammar had been his only concern, John could have used it in Jn 1:1. Except, of course, he had a higher goal than grammar.

grammatically and logically absurd. [11] It has to be explained before it makes sense. There is just no way to express readily in English what John was able to express in five words in Greek.

By using the form –

> *theos een ho logos*
> God was the Word

John was able to show that the Word was indeed God, but that there is still a distinction between the Word and the Father.

SECOND – THE SON IS NOT THE FATHER

> John's careful omission of *ho* from the second *theos* shows that the Word does not by himself make up the entire Godhead; yet the emphasis demanded by the inverted predicate shows that all the divinity of the Godhead still belongs to him. So the first *theos* with *ho* refers to God in his highest office, that is, to the Father; but the second *theos*, without *ho*, shows that while Christ has the nature and the essence of God, he is still distinct from the Father – that is, he is "*with* God." If *ho* had been added to the second *theos* then John would have been saying that Jesus is the Father, which is plainly false. [12]

---

(11) It is like saying, "that man stands beside himself", or that "this rock and the one next to it are the same rock". The scenario is impossible.

(12) This error is known as the *Sabellian* heresy. It first became prominent early in the third century, and was another attempt to solve the problem of maintaining the deity of Christ while at the same time holding to the unity of God. The Sabellians did this by arguing that Christ and the Holy Spirit were not separate persons

(continued on next page)

So John had to maintain both the full deity of Christ, and his distinction from the Father. He had to show that while the Logos is *equal* to the Father in nature and in being, he is *inferior* to the Father in office.

All of that he was able to do by carefully arranging the five words,

> *kai theos een ho logos*
> and God was the Word

In English, unfortunately, we have to translate the clause thus –

> "and the Word was God" (13)

(continued from previous page)

within the Godhead, but were simply different modes or expressions of the one God – as, for example, a king dealing with his son might behave as father, monarch, employer, judge, companion, or even enemy. Depending upon the circumstances he could present a variety of "faces" to his son, revealing a different aspect of himself for each occasion.

It is said that Tertullian mocked the Sabellians, saying they had "put the Holy Spirit to flight, and crucified the Father." A modern version of Sabellianism can be found in Unitarianism

(13) On the Arian argument that John's omission of the definite article requires the translation "a god", two other points should be noted – *(a)* it is true that normally "God" would be *ho theos*, and "a god" just *theos*; however, *(b)* the article can be omitted for some special reason (such as those I have indicated above), or because the context clearly identifies the person being described. Thus, in the Greek text of Ph 2:1 the phrase *"God the Father"* has no articles. Are we then to say that it should read, *"a god, a father"*? Similarly in Ro 15:32; 1 Co 14:2; 2 Co 1:2; Ga 4:7; etc., the article is missing from *theos* – yet in every case it is obvious that the reference is to God. The same applies to Jn 1:1, which by any fair translation practice, can be rendered in English only as *"The Word was God."*

a translation that shows well enough the deity of Christ, but remains ambiguous, lacking the subtlety and fine distinction John was able to convey in Greek.

THE MEANING OF "WITH"

On the clause, *"the Word was with God,"* Hendriksen says that the word "with" (*pros* in Greek) has the sense of being "face to face with God." He comments –

The meaning is that the Word existed (from the beginning) in the closest possible fellowship with the Father, and that he took supreme delight in this communion (cp. 1 Jn 1:2). So deeply had this former joy impressed itself upon the Logos that it was never erased from his consciousness, as is evident from the high-priestly prayer (Jn 17:5). Thus the incarnation begins to stand out more clearly as a deed of incomprehensible love and infinite condescension. [14]

And Arthur Gossip writes on the same passage –

> *The Christ of the NT is a figure so magnifical that whenever its writers think of him or name him, their minds instinctively bow down in reverence and worship. And the greatness of their Christ gives them a mighty gospel – this Christ who is the express image of God's person; in everything he does, God's representative; and himself divine; the very thought and mind and word of God to us has become alive here on our earth; the mighty conqueror of sin and death and hell, meeting the full shock of their power, and trampling them beneath his feet.*

---

(14) William Hendriksen, op.cit., pg. 71.

> *But often nowadays all that is whittled down into a tame affair, with little thrill in it, and with only a blunted cutting edge ... (But) we who have put him to the test know that the old staggering interpretation of him lies far nearer to the facts of our own experience – facts that cannot be ignored and that demand an explanation. It is a mighty gospel that Christ brings us, ample enough to cover every possible call upon it.* (15)

- **John 1:18** – "No one has ever seen God, but God the only Son, who is at the Father's side, has made him known" (NIV, NAB, and others).

Some critics (Alford and others) dispute this verse, claiming that the word "God" (*theos*) should be deleted from the middle clause (which would then simply read *"but the only Son"*).

However, Hendriksen says that the inclusion of *theos* is "supported by the best and oldest manuscripts." And Morris – "The reading (with *theos*) seems to have both better attestation and transcriptional probability on its side." And Bengel – "(*Theos* is) a striking variation, found in several of the best manuscripts and authorities."

If the opinion of those authorities is accepted, then John has here given us an unequivocal declaration of the deity of Christ, who is both God and Son.

THREE TITLES

It has been suggested that this verse gives three titles of Christ, and then summarises his ministry to us. His titles are – *God; The Only Son;* and *The One Who-Is-At-The-Father's-Side*.

---

(15) The Interpreter's Bible, Vol. 8, pg. 464.

His ministry is to make the Father known to us. He can do this, because he alone has truly and totally seen the Father. Others have seen the works of the Father, or have caught glimpses of his glory, but not even the holiest of the angels has ever fully seen God himself. But Christ is of the same being as the Father, and thus able to reveal the Father to all who desire that divine disclosure.

HOW DOES HE DO THIS?

Does Christ reveal the Father to us by showing us the Father apart from himself?

No. Rather, he does so by showing himself –

> He who has seen me has seen the Father. How can you say, "Show us the Father?" (Jn 14:9).

The Father will ever be visible to us only through his image reflected in Christ, who ...

> brightly reflects the glory of God, and is an exact representation of the being of God (He 1:3).

Arthur Way translates it –

> He is to God as the rays are which reveal to us all we know of the sun; he is the image that bodies out for us the essential being of God.

And G.H. Lang –

> Christ is the effulgence of God's glory, and the very image of his substance.

As the sun itself will never be seen by a human eye, but is visible to us only through its rays, so the Father "dwells in unapproachable light, whom no man has ever seen or can see" (1 Ti 6:16) – *but we see Christ, and in him the Father is made known.*

- **1 John 5:21** – "Little children, keep yourselves from idols."

Those are the last words in the letter. What a strange way to end it! So stark. So abrupt. It compels the reader to ask, "John, what are you talking about? Why this sudden warning against idolatry?"

Perhaps there is a clue in the previous verse? –

> We know that the Son of God has come and has given us understanding, to know him who is true; and we are in him who is true, in his Son Jesus Christ. This is the true God and eternal life (v. 20).

In that verse he talks about *"the true God,"* and in the next he warns, *"keep away from idols."* There is an inescapable connection between those two ideas. Perhaps he means, if we fail to understand who the true God is, then we may find ourselves worshipping a spurious God, thus making ourselves idolaters.

How then does he define the true God. How can we know just who is the true God?

John replies –

- only Jesus the Son of God can reveal the true God to us
- this, in fact, is why he came, so that we might *"know him who is true"* (that is, the true God)
- and through Christ, we have come into union with God so that we are now *"in him who is true"*
- but this union with God arises directly out of our union with Christ, for if we are *"in God"* it is only because we are *"in his Son Jesus Christ"*
- "this is the true God, and eternal life!"

WHO IS "THIS" TRUE GOD?

The word "this" is the pivot upon which the whole verse hangs – *"<u>This is the true God</u>."*

Does it refer to the Father only, and not to Christ; or to Christ only, and not the Father? Argument has raged furiously on that point across the centuries. Arians have vigorously insisted that the reference is only to the Father. The orthodox have just as strenuously contended that it must refer to Christ.

Who then is this *"true God"* – is he the Father? the Son? or both?

The various commentaries and critics I have been able to check are evenly divided on the matter – that is, they are divided on the question as to whether Greek grammar requires the word for *"this"* (houtos) to be applied to the clause that refers to *"Jesus Christ,"* or to the clause that refers to *"him who is true."*

THE FATHER AND THE SON TOGETHER ARE "THE TRUE GOD"

When experts disagree, where shall the humble stand? Since the grammatical problem exceeds my skills, I must rest upon common sense. And at once this becomes obvious to me – John was not intending to say either that the Father or the Son are exclusively *"the true God";* but rather, that we can understand *"the true God"* only when we see that <u>both</u> the Father <u>and</u> the Son are comprehended in God.

In other words, when he says, *"this is the true God, and eternal life,"* he means us to refer back to the whole of his previous statement, not just to one part of it. Now this statement begins with Jesus, and ends with Jesus, and the Father is at the centre of it –

- it begins with Jesus – "the Son of God has come"
- the Father is at the centre – "we know him who is true, and we are in him who is true"
- it ends with Jesus – "we are in his Son Jesus Christ"
    – "**<u>This</u>** (the whole of it) **<u>is the true God!</u>**"

It seems inconceivable to me that John could have so expressed himself, or so structured this verse, unless he was intending to affirm absolutely the full deity of both the Son and the Father.

BEWARE OF IDOLATRY!

Lest there should still be room for mistake, John adds the pungent finale, *"Keep yourselves from idols!"* That is, beware of worshipping anyone, including Jesus, who is less than God. If Christ is not fully God, then to worship him is idolatry; and it is also futile, for God alone has the attribute of omnipresence that makes worship meaningful.

To say that Christ is not God is idolatry. To exalt Christ above the Father is idolatry. But to understand that Jesus reveals the Father, that we come into union with the Father through our union with Christ, that to know the Son is to know the Father, and that to know the Father is to know the Son – <u>*this is indeed the true God, and eternal life*</u>!

- Romans 9:5

An exact translation of Paul's original Greek would read like this –

> (From Israel comes) the Christ according to the flesh the one being over all God praised unto the ages amen (there is no punctuation in the original Greek manuscripts of the NT.)

Now before that can make any sense in English it has to be punctuated – and at once the quarrel begins, because the choice of punctuation can radically alter its meaning.

There are a number of options, but overwhelmingly translators choose either one of these two –

> (From Israel comes) the Christ, according to the flesh. May God who is over all be praised for ever. Amen.

> (From Israel comes) the Christ, according to the flesh, who is God over all, for ever praised. Amen.

In the first of those translations, a full-stop is placed after "flesh," and the remainder of the verse is a simple doxology, praising God, and containing no reference to the deity of Christ.

In the second, a comma is placed after "flesh," and the remainder of the verse is both an ascription of praise to Christ, and a bold affirmation of his deity.

Which of those two versions is correct?

A DOXOLOGY TO CHRIST

It must be insisted that from a purely grammatical point of view, both translations are fully permissible. There is no way of determining from the Greek text itself just how the verse should be punctuated. The choice of punctuation has to be made on other linguistic or doctrinal grounds, and sincere people hold different opinions about the various arguments.

So there are some who insist it is wrong to translate the last part of the verse as a doxology, because Paul does not use the standard form of a doxology; the word order usual for a doxology has been changed.

Furthermore (they say), he uses the same kind of terminology as John used (1:1) – that is, instead of employing the form *ho theos,* he simply writes *theos* (see my comments above on Jn 1:1.)

If Paul had been intending to write a doxology to God the Father – so the argument goes – he would certainly have written *ho theos*. His use of *theos* (without the definite article) indicates Christ, who possesses the essence of God, but is inferior to the Father in office (though not in person). Hence the second translation is correct –

> "Christ, who is God over all, for ever praised!"

Thus we have here a plain statement that Christ is God.

A DOXOLOGY TO THE FATHER

But others contend that such language is unnatural for Paul. He nowhere else so clearly calls Christ God; yet if this phraseology was natural to him, surely he would have used it in other places? The argument continues – it is also noteworthy that a number of ancient Greek copies of the NT do place a period after "flesh," thus requiring the last part of the verse to be a doxology to God.

Hence the first translation is correct –

"May God who is over all be praised for ever!"

In that case, there is no ascription of deity to Christ.

WAS PAUL TOO CARELESS?

Many other arguments have been gathered by both sides, and it must be allowed that personal disposition, rather than irrefutable proof, is likely to be the main factor determining which translation each reader will prefer. In the words of F.F. Bruce, "it is outrageous to cast doubt on the orthodoxy of those translators or commentators who prefer" one translation or the other.

The fact is, the Greek text as it stands, without punctuation (as it would have been when Paul wrote it), is as ambiguous as its unpunctuated English translation.

What then are we to do with it?

Must we accuse Paul of being careless? Could he really have written so ambiguously unless he actually intended to do so?

It does seem incredible to suppose Paul would write a sentence, in which he surely knew many people would see a declaration of the deity of Christ, unless he himself actually did believe that Christ and God are one.

The fact is, if Christ is not God, then he must be a creature of God, and between the Creator and the creature, even the highest creature, there is a gulf so vast that any confusion of the Maker with the made is blasphemy. If Paul had thought of Christ as a being created by God, even though a divine being, he could not possibly have left himself open to the accusation that he had called Christ God.

I think it is better to suppose that Paul wrote carefully, and that he knew very well what he was saying. He knew that his words were open to two different meanings, and I suggest he probably intended that very thing. He wanted his words to convey the two ideas – a statement of Christ's deity; and a doxology in praise of God.

At any rate, it seems that any attempt to say the latter part of *Romans 9:5* must be exclusively read either as a doxology or as a statement of Christ's deity, reflects prejudice more than proof.

For my part, since Paul may be correctly understood as writing "Christ is God over all," and since it would be unbelievably careless of him to leave his words open to this reading if Christ is *not* "God over all," I am convinced he did indeed believe in the full deity of Christ.

In other words, whether or not Paul actually intended to write these words in *Romans 9:5*, he certainly could have written them, there or anywhere – *"Christ is God over all, for ever praised! Amen."*

THERE ARE TOO MANY TREASURES!

I feel as though I could go on writing for ever on this magnificent theme, but I have already exceeded the set limits for this part of our study. Yet there are so many intriguing passages!

How much I could say, for example, about these breathtaking declarations –

> In Christ all things were created, in heaven and on earth, visible and invisible, whether thrones

or dominions or principalities or authorities – all things were created through him and for him ... For in him the whole fulness of deity dwells bodily (Cl 1:15-16; 2:9).

And what a powerful argument could be built around statements like these –

" ... according to the grace of our God and Lord, Jesus Christ" (2 Th 1:12).

" ... the glory of our great God and Saviour Jesus Christ" (Tit 2:11).

" ... the righteousness of our God and Saviour Jesus Christ" (2 Pe 1:1). [16]

In the first of those three passages (2 Th 1:12)

there is an article before 'our God' and none before 'Lord Jesus Christ', hence it is grammatically possible to understand the expression to mean, 'our God and Lord, Jesus Christ' ... (Even if that translation is disallowed) we should not overlook the fact that Paul does link them (God and Christ) very closely indeed. The fact that there can be this doubt as to whether one or both is meant is indicative of the closeness of their connection

---

(16) Concerning this third passage (2 Pe 1:1), Alford admits that "in strict grammatical propriety" the nouns "God" and "Saviour" are both predicates of "Jesus Christ" – hence the translation I have given above (from the RSV) is perfectly correct. He argues against this translation (as he did for *Titus 2:13*, which has an identical Greek structure), but has to do so on grounds other than the grammar of the verse.

> *in the mind of Paul. He makes no great distinction between them.* (17)

Concerning the second passage (Tit 2:13), Alford argues that it should be translated: *" ... the glory of our great God, and of our Saviour Jesus Christ"* – that is, he separates God and Christ. However, he then declares that whichever way the passage is taken, "it is just as important a testimony to the divinity of our Saviour." For if the translation I have given above is followed, then Christ is plainly declared to be *"our great God and Saviour"* Alford however, reckons that his translation shows the deity of Christ "even more strikingly (by) asserting his equality in glory with the Father, in a way which would be blasphemy if predicated of any of the sons of men." (18)

Many other exegetes and translators (including most of those in my library) argue strongly for the translation I have given above (from the RSV), which indicates that Christ and God are one person.

However, no grammatical arguments about the best way to translate those statements can alter their extraordinary impact, which is one of placing Christ at the pinnacle of power and glory. How could God-fearing men make such statements unless they were profoundly convinced that God and Christ are one? And there are many more such passages. What I have written thus far is really hardly more than an introduction to the subject.

---

(17) Leon Morris, *in loc.*, <u>The New International Commentary on the New Testament</u>. Dr Morris himself prefers the translation: " *... according to the grace of our God and the Lord Jesus Christ"* - an English rendering which contains the same kind of ambiguity as Paul's Greek.)

(18) *Op. cit., in loc.*

But it is time to move on from this part of our discussion, and to consider the opinions about Christ held by those who came after the apostles – the Church Fathers. That will be the theme of our next chapter, along with a look at the miracles of Christ, and what his deity means to us who believe.

Chapter Three

THE WITNESS OF HIS MIRACLES

In our quest for proof of the deity of Christ we call on two more witnesses – the miracles Jesus did; and the testimony of the Church Fathers. Then we will conclude with a look at the immense value we gain from seeing Christ as both Son of God and Son of Man.

DO MIRACLES PROVE THE DEITY OF CHRIST?

When proofs are required of the deity of Christ, many people refer at once to his miracles – healing the sick, casting out demons, raising the dead, hushing the storm, riding the wild ass, and so on.

Those miracles certainly show that God was with Christ, but are they really a demonstration of deity?

- John calls the miracles of Christ "signs"

See John 1:11,23; 3:2; 4:54; 6:2; etc.

Likewise, the man who was born blind, after he had been healed by Jesus, said to the Pharisees, *"If this man (Jesus) were not from God he could do nothing"* (Jn 9:33).

Thus it is claimed that Jesus' miracles show that he was sent by God, and that he was not acting disobediently to the will of God (vs 30-31); but it cannot be claimed that they show he had a divine nature. Jesus himself promised that his disciples would also perform amazing miracles (Mk 16:17-20; Jn 14:12), but this did not lead them to claim personal divinity.

So also Paul, and others of the early preachers, wrought many signs and wonders (Ro 15:18-19; He 2:3-4; etc.), but no one ever thought to call them gods (except for the dramatic incident at Lystra – Ac 14:8-15). The fact is, power to work miracles may be communicated to any person by the Holy Spirit. This communicated power may show that the miracle-worker is a true servant of God, but it cannot by itself show that the miracle-worker has a divine nature.

- John says that Jesus' glory was manifested by his miracles – John 1:14; 2:11.

That is, of course, true, but it was only to his disciples. Other people had a very mixed response to his mighty works – some refused to believe they had actually happened; others said he was in league with Satan; some thought he might be one of the ancient prophets reincarnated; others feared and hated him.

Many of Jesus' miracles – even those with a "creative" element – are parallelled by OT miracles – cp. *John 2:7-10; Matthew 8:26; John 6:11; 11:43-44;* etc., with *1 Kings 17:20-24; 2 Kings 4:1-7, 42-44; 6:1-7;* etc. There is no thought of attributing deity to the agents of those earlier signs.

- Jesus often wanted his miracles kept unknown.

He realised that they would not by themselves convince many people of his identity, and that too much furore about them would hinder his teaching ministry and perhaps precipitate violence (Mt 9:30; Mk 9:25; etc.).

- The miracles of Jesus are expressly attributed to the communicated power of the Holy Spirit.

See *Acts 10:38; Luke 4:18*; thus they do not by themselves establish his deity, although they certainly do confirm that he was the One predicted by the prophets (Lu 4:16-21).

THE RESURRECTION AND THE DEITY OF CHRIST

RAISED BY HIS OWN POWER

If other miracles remain inconclusive, there is certainly one that is an unassailable proof that Jesus is God – *the miracle of his resurrection.*

Jesus himself made this astonishing claim –

> No one takes my life from me, but I lay it down
> of my own accord. I have power to lay it down,
> and I have power to take it up again! (Jn.10:18)

No other man who has ever lived has been so bold! No wonder, when they heard such words, many of the Jews exclaimed, *"He has a demon, and he is mad! Why listen to him?"* To claim power to raise himself from the dead was either the raving of a deluded mind, or the simple truth spoken by One who knew he had absolute authority over death – and who else is that but God?

He did indeed lay down his life. That was not remarkable. Many martyrs have done as much. No one believed at that time that his life could not be taken against his will. But three days later the empty tomb showed for all time that this *"Jesus of Nazareth, the King of the Jews"* was unlike any other man who has ever lived. He truly did lay down his life – it was not taken from him. He *did* have power to take back his life again, and to raise himself from the dead! By this he showed himself to be truly *Son of God* as well as *Son of Man*.

That is why Paul wrote –

> Our Lord Jesus Christ, in his human nature, was a descendant of David; but then he was shown to be the Son of God with power, according to the Spirit of holiness, by his resurrection from the dead. (Ro 1:3-4)

Note: he did not *become* the Son of God by his resurrection; rather, the resurrection "designated" or "declared" or "revealed" him to be the Son of God. The resurrection was the climax of his miracles and gave authenticity and an enlarged significance to all the others.

Without the resurrection, doubt would have remained about whether or not Jesus was the Messiah, or merely a prophet, or perhaps even a deceiver (cp. Mt 16:13-17; 24:23-24). So there were some who argued that his miracles were done by demon-power; while others retorted, *"Can a demon open the eyes of the blind?"* (Jn 10:21).

But Jesus' triumph over death finally removed all doubt. Thereafter, the debate was silenced in favour of those (like the blind man, 9:30-33) who had believed that his miracles proved he came from God.

HIS RESURRECTION VALIDATES ALL HIS MIRACLES

Because of the resurrection, Peter was able to declare boldly –

> *You people of Israel, mark these words – Jesus of Nazareth was a man endorsed by God with mighty works, wonders, and signs that God publicly did through him. (Ac 2:22)*

But that "endorsement" did not become truly valid until it was completed by the resurrection (vs 24, 32-33), which at once gave an entirely different character to all his other miracles. Before the resurrection they were at best the signs of a prophet sent by God; but now the resurrection shows those former works to have been signs of the Son of God.

This leads to another way in which Jesus' earlier miracles can be seen as proof of his deity. If I should perform miracles in the name of the Father, that would not prove I am the Son of God, nor that I have a divine nature. But then I am not claiming to be the Son of God, and if I did make such a claim the Father would soon withdraw his Spirit from me, and I would lose all the power to work miracles.

But Jesus, as we have already seen, did claim many divine prerogatives, and so aroused the hatred of the Jews, who accused him of foul blasphemy. Their accusation would have been reasonable, except for one thing – *no matter how fantastic the things he said seemed to be, the Father did not withdraw from him!*

On the contrary, the power of God in Christ waxed ever more mighty. Jesus insisted that his enemies should face this fact, and scornfully denounced them because they refused to do so (Mt 12:25-32; Jn 10:24-26, 31-39). He allowed that they would have had reason to be offended by his *words* if they had not also been witnesses of his *works*. But since they had seen many astounding things done by him in the name of the Father, they were guilty of wilful unbelief and inexcusable blasphemy against the Holy Spirit (cp. also Jn 3:2; 5:36; 12:37-40; 14:10; 15:24; Mt 11:20-24).

So all the miracles of Jesus, when they are placed within the frame of his teaching and of his resurrection, become proofs of his deity – for if he were not what he claimed to be, then the Father would not have approved him by mighty signs and wonders, and his body would have remained in the grave.

Chapter Four

THE WITNESS OF THE FATHERS

Although there were a few dissenting voices, the majority of church leaders in the century following the apostles were convinced that Christ is God. Their testimony is decisive, because they lived in the same cultural milieu as the apostles, they spoke the same language, they stood in direct line of descent to the apostles, and they had no doubt that the writings of the apostles gave eloquent testimony of the deity of Christ.

I have culled the following paragraphs from the writings of the Fathers. These examples are far from being complete (they could be multiplied several times), but they are sufficient to show how early and how firmly the deity of Christ became part of the fixed dogma of the church So they stand in direct contrast to people who try to show that the doctrine of the deity of Christ was a late innovation in Christian belief, and that he is a divine person, but not God. [19].

The selections are placed in order of date, not order of merit, and they represent the thinking of the Church Fathers of the second and third centuries (AD 100-200).

- ***"The Letter of Barnabas"*** (anonymous, c. 100)

    (Christ) is, after all, the Lord of all the earth, to whom at the foundation of the world God had

---

(19)   Such as Jehovah's Witnesses; Unitarians; Christadelphians; Oneness Pentecostals; and others.

addressed the words, "Let us make man, in our image and likeness." [20]

- **_Ignatius, bishop of Antioch_** (c. 112), "Letter to the Ephesians" (7:2)

    There is one Physician, fleshly and spiritual, begotten and unbegotten, God in man, true life in death, both of Mary and of God, first passible then impassible, Jesus Christ our Lord. [21]

- **_"The Letter to Diognetus"_** (anonymous, c. 124)

    (God did not), as one might imagine, send to mankind some servant of his, some angel or prince; it is none of the great ones of the earth, nor even one of the vice-regents of heaven. It is no other than the Universal Artificer and Constructor himself, by whose agency God made the heavens and set the seas in their bounds, whose mystic words the elements of creation submissively obey ... Ordainer, Disposer, and the Ruler of all things is he; of heaven and all that heaven holds, of earth and all that is in earth, of sea and every creature

---

(20)   Part One, Ch. 5; ANF Vol. One, *in loc.*

(21)   Tr. by Maxwell Staniforth, <u>Early Christian Writings</u>; Penguin Books, 1968. "Passible" means "able to suffer, or to feel emotion"; "impassible" means "unable to feel pain, to be harmed, to feel emotion, to be moved by passion, without sensation". Some scholars accept the doctrine of the "impassibility" of Christ; others, myself included, reject it, because there are too many scriptures that speak about divine pleasure, anger, love, joy, and the like. But much depends upon how far the definition of "impassible" is pressed. If it is limited in meaning, then it can be accepted. See below, in *Chapter Seven* under *Final Propositions*.

therein; of fires, ether, and the bottomless pit; of things above and things below, and things in the midst ... As a king sending his royal son, so sent he him; *as God he sent him* ... (1:7). [22]

- ***"The Second Letter of Clement"*** (anonymous, c. 140)

  Brethren it is fitting that you should think of Jesus Christ as of God – as the Judge of the living and the dead ... for if we think little of him, we shall also hope to obtain but little from him (ch. 1). [23]

(This "letter" is thought actually to be the transcript of a sermon, the oldest sermon, apart from those in the NT, still extant. It begins with the words quoted.)

- ***Justin Martyr***, apologist (c. 150); "Dialogue With Trypho"

  (Jesus is called) Christ and God ... For if you had understood what has been written by the prophets, you would not have denied that he was God, Son of the only, unbegotten, unutterable God (ch. 126). [24]

- ***Irenaeus***, bishop of Lyons (c. 180); "Against Heresies"

  ... Christ Jesus (is) our Lord, and God, and Saviour, and King, according to the will of the invisible Father (1:10) ... Then Paul quotes *Romans 9:5*, "(Christ) is God over all, blessed for ever" (3:16) ... I have shown that the Son of

---

(22) ANF Vol. Nine, *in loc.*
(23) ANF Vol. One, *in loc.*
(24) *Ibid.*

> God did not then begin to exist (when he was born of Mary), for he has existed with the Father from the very beginning (3:18) ... I have shown from the scriptures that no son of Adam has ever been, in everything, or absolutely, called God, or named Lord. But that Christ himself, in his own right, and above all men who ever lived, is God and Lord and King Eternal, and the Incarnate Word ... may be seen by all who have attained to even a small portion of the truth (3:19). [25]

The testimony of Irenaeus is particularly significant, because he was a godly, zealous, yet gracious (as his popular name implies) defender of apostolic doctrines (as he saw them).

- **_Gaius_**, presbyter of Rome (c. 200), "Against Artemon"

   > ... there are the writings of certain (earlier) brethren ... which they wrote against the heathen in defence of the truth, and against the heresies of their time – I mean Justin, and Miltiades, and Tatian, and Clement, and many others, in all which divinity is ascribed to Christ. For who is ignorant of the books of Irenaeus, and Melito, and the rest, which declare Christ to be God and man? All the psalms, too, and hymns of brethren, which have been written from the beginning by the faithful, celebrate Christ the Word of God, ascribing divinity to him. Since the doctrine of the Church, then, has been proclaimed so many

---

(25) The reference numbers in brackets (except for the scripture reference) are to book and chapter numbers in <u>Against Heresies</u>. (ANF, Vol. One, *in loc.*)

years ago, how is it possible that men have preached ... this God-denying apostasy ... that Christ was a mere man? (sec. 1). [26]

- ***Tertullian***, apologist (c. 200), "Against Praxeas"

    ... I shall follow the (example of the) apostles; so that if the Father and the Son are alike to be invoked, I shall call the Father "God", and invoke Jesus Christ as "Lord". But when Christ alone is mentioned, I shall be able to call him "God" (ch. 13).

    ... What need would there be of the gospel ... (if) the Father, the Son, and the Spirit are not believed in, both as Three, and as making One Only God? (ch. 31). [27]

- ***Origen***, Alexandrian theologian (c. 220), "Contra Celsus"

    We worship, therefore, the Father of truth, and the Son, who is the truth; and these, while they are two, considered as persons or subsistences, are one in unity of thought, in harmony, and in identity of will. So entirely are they one, that he who has seen the Son, *"who is the brightness of God's glory, and the express image of his person,"* has seen in him who is the image of God, God himself (ch. 12). [28]

    ... divesting himself of his glory, (Christ) became a man, and was incarnate although

---

(26) Eusebius, Ecclesiastical History, Bk 5, Ch 28; Baker Book House, Grand Rapids, Michigan; 1977; pg. 213.
(27) ANF Vol. Three, *in loc.*
(28) ANF Vol. Four, *in loc.*

God, and while made a man remained the God which he was (De Principiis, *Pref.* 4). (29)

The omnipotence of the Father and the Son is one and the same ... listen to the manner in which John speaks in the Apocalypse – 'Thus saith the Lord God, which is, and which was, and which is to come, the Almighty' (Re 1:8). For who else was 'he which is to come' than Christ? And as no one ought to be offended, seeing God is the Father, that the Saviour is also God; so also, since the Father is called omnipotent, no one ought to be offended that the Son of God is also called omnipotent (Bk. 3, ch. 2, par. 10). (30)

- **_Novatian_**, presbyter of Rome (c. 250). Although Novatian flourished in the middle of the third century, his great work "De Trinitate" was the first full length treatment of the Trinity (31) ever presented to the

---

(29)   Ibid.
(30)   Ibid.
(31)   The earliest known use of the word "Trinity" occurs in a 2nd-cent work, Theophilus to Autolycus – "For the sun is a type of God, and the moon of man. And as the sun far surpasses the moon in power and glory, so far does God surpass man. And as the sun remains ever full, never becoming less, so does God always abide perfect, being full of all power, and understanding, and wisdom, and immortality, and all good. But the moon wanes monthly, and in a manner dies, being a type of man; then it is born again, and is crescent, for a pattern of the future resurrection. In like manner also the three days which were before the luminaries, are types of the Trinity, of God, and His Word, and His wisdom." (Bk. II, Ch. 15; emphasis mine) (ANF Vol. Two, in loc.) Theophilus was the 6th bishop of Antioch. The quotation comes from a screed he wrote circa 180 to a pagan friend, hoping to convert him to Christianity. Plainly, though, the word was not invented by Theophilus. His manner of introducing

(continued on next page)

Western Church. It brought together in a formal treatise all that had, during the previous (second) century, come to represent orthodox doctrine on the Godhead –

> But lest ... we should seem to have given assent to other heretics, who ... maintain that (Christ) is man only and alone, and therefore desire to prove that he was a man bare and solitary ... we do not so express doctrine concerning the substance of his body as to say that he is only and alone man, but so as to maintain, by the association of the divinity of the Word in that very materiality, that he was also God according to the scriptures.
>
> ... there is a great risk of saying that the Saviour of the human race was only man ... and denying to him divine authority .. For scripture as much announces Christ as also God, as it announces God himself as man. It has as much described Jesus Christ to be man, as moreover it has also described Christ the Lord to be God.
>
> For as nature itself has prescribed that he must be believed to be a man who is of man, so the same nature prescribes also that he must be believed to be God who is of God; but if he should not also be God when he is of God, no more should he be man although he should be of man. And thus both doctrines would be endangered in one and the other way, by one being convicted to have lost belief in the other.

(continued from previous page)

it, without comment, suggests that "Trinity" was already in fairly common use, at least among scholars and probably also the clergy, if not lay people.

Let them, therefore, who read that Jesus Christ the Son of man is man, read also that this same Jesus is called also God and the Son of God (ch. 11). [32]

THE IMPORTANCE OF THIS WITNESS

Selections such as those above leave us in no doubt that belief in the deity of Christ was accepted as orthodox doctrine by those who were teachers of the church immediately after the apostles.

The Fathers did state this doctrine more emphatically than the apostles had, and they certainly developed it further – but in all their writings there is confidence they were teaching nothing more than the apostolic doctrine. It was taken for granted that the deity of Christ is either clearly stated or at least implied on nearly every page of the gospels and letters.

It is difficult to explain this almost unanimous early Christian belief in the deity of Christ, except by assuming this doctrine had been taught to the previous generation by the apostles themselves. Thus, before the death of the last of the apostles, recognition of Jesus as God had already become widely established in the church.

---

(32)   ANF Vol. 5, *in loc.*

Chapter Five

EXTRAORDINARY BENEFITS

The purpose of Christian doctrine is never finally to say something about *God*, but rather to say something about *man*. Every article of our faith turns eventually toward us and reveals some new benefit that Divine grace offers us.

So with this doctrine of the deity of Christ.

It is given to us by God in scripture, not to promote his own glory (although it does do that), but rather to promote *our* salvation, to strengthen *our* assurance, to enlarge *our* hope, and to compel *our* obedience.

Here are a few of the special values you can gain from this great doctrine –

WE ARE NOT ALONE

One of the most poignant sorrows of being human is the intense sense of loneliness, of isolation, that every person experiences.

We feel alone within **ourselves**, because our fractured self-awareness prevents us from truly grasping our personal identity; we are strangers to our own nature.

We feel alone in **society**, because there is finally an uncrossable gulf that isolates each of us from each other. In the end we are strangers even to those we love most deeply. Despite our most earnest efforts, we are unable to bridge the hiatus that lies between all human souls; we are unable fully to communicate one with the other.

Worst of all, we feel alone in the **universe**. The whole race of man is a stranger to the entire cosmos. Across countless generations sensitive men and women have searched the skies above them for a Friend, only to conclude that they were lost, and alone.

Coleridge, under the guise of the *Ancient Mariner*, depicted this awful sense of estrangement –

> Alone, alone, all, all alone;
> Alone, on a wide, wide sea!
> And never a saint took pity on
>
> My soul in agony. ...
> Alone on a wide wide sea:
> So lonely 'twas, that God himself
> Scarce seemed there to be. (33)

Or perhaps the dolorous words of Fiona McLeod –

> Deep in the heart of Summer,
> Sweet is life to me still,
> My heart is a lonely hunter
> That hunts on a lonely hill. (34)

But I cannot find any better expression of this alone-ness than the words of the ninth century poet, Ono No Komachi –

> So lonely am I
> My body is a floating weed
> Severed at the roots.
> Were there water to entice me,
> I would follow it, I think. (35)

---

(33) *The Rime of the Ancient Mariner* (1798); Part Four, stanza 3; Part Seven, stanza 19.

(34) "Fiona MacLeod" was a pseudonym of the Scottish writer, William Sharp (1855-1905). Poem, *The Lonely Hunter*, stanzas 3 and 6.

(35) Komachi was probably a lady in waiting in the court of a Japanese emperor. Her poem comes from an anthology published by imperial command in 905 A.D., known as <u>A Collection of Anciant and Modern Poems</u>.

"I think!" There is man's dilemma. He is so far estranged from himself, his neighbours, and his world, he is not sure he would welcome a Friend, even if he should find one!

But into this loneliness Christ has come. *"Emmanuel"* – *"God with us!"* Whether people welcome this Christ or not, they can never again lament that they are alone. God has invaded the world. The cosmos is not empty, but is full of Christ (Ep 1:23; Cl 1:15-19). The gap is bridged. The vacuum is filled. He is everywhere and with everyone, through all time and into eternity. God is not infinitely remote, but intensely imminent in Christ. Through him I can find friendship with myself, communication with my neighbour, and union with the divine. As he is one with the Father, so I can become one with him, and through this unity find that the breaching of my personal and social life has been marvellously mended.

I was lonely. But because God has come to me in Christ, I am alone no more!

GOD CARES FOR YOU

Before the appearance of Christ, it was easy enough to believe that God *existed*, but not so easy to believe that God *cared*. For most people, in ancient times, and also today, Emily Dickinson's petulant lines express God's seeming indifference –

> Of Course – I prayed –
> And did God Care?
> He cared as much as on the Air
> A Bird – had stamped her foot –
> And cried, 'Give Me.' ...
> 'Twere better Charity
> To leave me in the Atom's Tomb —

> Merry, and Nought, and gay, and numb —
> Than this smart Misery. [36]

But there is no more any place for such cynicism. God's actions in Christ show that he *does* care. No more can anyone say, "Why doesn't God *do* something?" God *has* done something. He has acted in Christ to create for us perfect pardon for all sin and perfect life in his eternal kingdom. If he never did another thing, if he never answered another prayer, he has already done enough to show that he cares more than we shall ever know.

God walked this world in the person of Christ.

In Christ, God wept; he was hungry and thirsty; he slept; he was lonely and weary.

In Christ, God shared the pangs of death.

How then could I say, *"He does not care?"* He did not send an angel, *but came himself.*

If Christ were another, and not truly "Emmanuel," then I could perhaps wonder whether God's concern for me might not be artificial? But how can I doubt his love when I know that he has been where I am? He has felt my pain. The horror of death has shadowed his soul. The taste of sin has poisoned his spirit and slain his flesh (2 Co 5:21). God was in Christ reconciling me to himself. Oh! he cares!

YOU MAY FREELY WORSHIP CHRIST

Suppose Jesus is not God? Suppose he is only some kind of superior angel, the highest thing in all creation perhaps, but

---

(36) <u>The Poems of Emily Dickinson</u>; RW Franklin; Belknap Press, Cambridge; 1999; Poem 376. Emily Dickinson (1839-1886) was an American writer whose work was largely ignored until after her death. She is now reckoned as a major poet.

still a creature and not the Creator? How different religious life would be! Neither you nor I could follow our natural instincts toward Christ – those instincts that arise out of our deep sense of union with him, and the urge to express praise and gratitude to him.

You could not _worship_ him, for if he is not God, then to fall down before him would be idolatry.

You could not _commune_ with him, because prayer is meaningful only when it is addressed to God, who alone has the capacity to hear and answer your petitions, along with those of every other human soul.

You could not be _strengthened_ by him, for if he were but an enlarged man, his power and his ability to help you would not be adequate. Only God can do all that needs to be done to enable you to fulfil heaven's eternal purpose. Omnipotence is a divine attribute. No creature, no matter how exalted, can possess it.

If Christ is just a creature of God, then he is essentially the same sort of being as I am, and it was no special act of grace on his part to assume human form. Like the angel who rebuked the prostrate John, if I attempted to fall at Jesus' feet and worship him (if he is not God), he would have to say to me,

> *You must not do that! For I am a fellow servant with you and your brethren the prophets, and with those who keep the words of this book. Worship God! (Re 22:8-9).*

But there is no such rebuke in scripture for those who fall at Jesus' feet. There is no restraint placed on the exuberance of their joy nor on their praise of him. On the contrary, the saints are vigorously urged to lift their voices in his worship, to acclaim him loudly, to exalt his holy name! (Re 5:9-14).

Whatever some Christian _heads_ might say, all Christian _hearts_ yearn to glorify Christ, to give him the highest possible honour, to fellowship with him at all times and in every place, to live in intimate union with him. Yet all of this would be impossible if you and I could not cry out to him, as Thomas did,

"My Lord and my God!"

Many years ago I dabbled briefly in the Arian heresy.[37] But I soon discovered a major problem. My heart was embarrassed by its love for Christ and its desire to rejoice in him. The voice of praise was strangled in me. Arian dogma allowed me to offer him honour and gratitude, as I might to any other man or angel who had done some great thing for me, but nothing more. Yet my heart yearned to give Jesus adoration, worship, and praise. But if he is not God then such behaviour would make me an idolater!

Then I discovered his real identity!

The fetters broke away from my soul; and now I am free to exalt him, and to abandon myself to his love!

HE MAKES GOD REAL

The image of God in the OT is vague. Even Moses (the man of whom it was said, *"The Lord used to speak to Moses face to face, as a man speaks to his friend"*) in the end was given only a veiled glimpse –

> *(The Lord said to Moses), "You cannot see my face; for man shall not see me and live ... Behold, there is a place by me where you shall stand upon the rock; and while my glory passes by I will put you in a cleft of the rock, and I will cover you with my hand until I have passed by; then I will take away my hand, and*

---

(37)　See *Chapter Seven*, under the heading "Ancient Heresies – #3, Arianism".

you shall see my back; but my face shall not be seen." (Ex 33:11, 20-23).

Thinkers about God used to wonder if he is really a "Person," or perhaps just a "Being," an "Essence," a "Source"? Does he "think" and "feel"? Is he aloof from all emotion, all pain? Does he look upon men and women compassionately or dispassionately?

It must be allowed that the general evidence of life around us might lead people to conclude that "God", if he exists, is some kind of indifferent, apathetic Power, lacking any traits of warm and vital personality.

The psalmist could sing, "the heavens declare the glory of God, and the firmament proclaims his handiwork;" and Paul could claim that the physical creation reveals God's "invisible nature, along with his eternal power and deity"; but they could not say that those things pictured God as a loving Father (Ps 19:1; Ro 1:19-20).

But then Christ came. The image of God was "fleshed out" – suddenly, human perception of God was radically changed. The Father became warmly personal.

Whereas in the OT he is not once specifically addressed as "Father," [38] we now address him in this fashion more than

---

(38) Possible exceptions are Is 63:16; 64:8, although in both cases "Father" is used as a *description* of God rather than as a personal *name*. The same is true of the other OT references to the Fatherhood of God (taken from Strong's Concordance) – 2 Sa 7:14; 1 Ch 17:13; 22:10; 28:6; 29:10(?); Ps 68:5; 89:26; 103:13; Pr 3:12; Is 9:6; Je 3:4,19; 31:19; Mal 1:6; 2:10 – which I think is a complete list; except that to this list there should probably be added those references that speak of Israel as *"sons," "daughters,"* or *"children,"* of God.

Those references all lack the personal element *"Father"* is given in the NT. The sense of the OT references is more that of national Creator than it is of family Friend. God is the "Father" of

(continued on next page)

any other. Jesus taught us to say, *"My Father!"* and then showed us in himself what the Father is like (Jn 14:8-11).

Of course, God has lost none of his majesty, and I am still constrained to bow before him in reverent awe. But through Christ, God has also become *"Father"* – vividly personal, intimately loving, warmly real, tenderly caring, easily approachable, and very, very near.

HE DESERVES ALL YOUR TRUST AND OBEDIENCE

The more highly Christ is exalted, the more deeply it is possible to trust him, and the more earnestly to obey him. Total trust. Complete obedience. Those two things inevitably

---

(continued from previous page)

> Israel in the sense of being the Founder of the nation, its Protector and Redeemer; there is little suggestion of the intimate family association given to *"Father"* in the NT. "Father" in the OT has the same connotation as "Sire" when used of an English king, who was seen as the "Father" of the nation.
>
> In the OT, *"Father"* is also used in special connection with the House of David (2 Sa 7:14; etc.). Here again, the sense is more that of family Ancestor and Mentor than of a warmly personal, deeply caring Friend.
>
> Perhaps, however, it might be more accurate to say, not that the OT use of *"Father"* is actually impersonal, but that Israel failed to realise the personal significance that lay behind this appellation. It is evident from a general reading of the OT that the people of Israel were reluctant to address God directly as *"Father."* They probably felt that such intimacy would be presumptuous. Yet it is just as evident that God kept on trying to show himself to them in this capacity, and to draw from them a loving response to his personal fatherhood – *"I thought you would call me, 'My Father' ... "* (Je 3:19). But no man was ever bold enough to speak to God that way – until Jesus came. Only through the example and teaching of Christ do the OT references to God as *"Father"* gain their full personal significance.

flow out of an affirmation that *"Jesus is Lord!"* To the extent that his glory is denigrated or his authority is diminished, to that extent we undermine the basis of our own faith and weaken the necessity to serve him.

But let such ideas be far from you! With Thomas let us fall at his feet, crying, *"My Lord and my God!"* And when I say, *"My Lord,"* I am saying, "I will serve you for ever!" And when I say, *"My God,"* I am saying, "In you only, blessed Saviour, do I put my trust!"

May that great affirmation be yours also.

Chapter Six

CREEDS AND CANONS

In the year of our Lord 451, after four centuries of furious debate about the nature of Christ, some 400 bishops, prelates, and other dignitaries assembled in holy council at Chalcedon, determined to create a formula acceptable to all churches.

The longed-for unity was not achieved. For Chalcedon, instead of healing the divisions among Christians, made some of the rifts so deep they still endure today.

However, Chalcedon did produce a ponderous formula, which has been (and is) accepted by *most* churches as an adequate summary of the true doctrine of Christ. It is known as *The Definition of Chalcedon*, and it says –

THE DEFINITION OF CHALCEDON

> Therefore, following the holy fathers, we all with one accord teach men to acknowledge one and the same Son, our Lord Jesus Christ, at once complete in godhead and complete in manhood, truly God and truly man, consisting also of a reasonable soul and body; of one substance with the Father as regards his godhead, and at the same time of one substance with us as regards his manhood; like us in all respects, apart from sin; as regards his godhead, begotten of the Father before the ages; but as regards his manhood, begotten, for us men and for our salvation, of Mary the Virgin, the God-bearer; one and the same Christ, Son, Lord, Only-begotten, recognised in two natures, without confusion, without

> change, without division, without separation; the distinction of natures in no way being annulled by the union, but rather the characteristics of each nature being preserved and coming together to form one person and subsistence, not as parted or separated into two persons, but one and the same Son and Only-begotten God the Word, the Lord Jesus Christ; even as the prophets from earliest times spoke of him, and our Lord Jesus Christ himself taught us, and the creed of the Fathers has handed down to us. (39)

What "the prophets, the gospels, the creeds, and Jesus himself" are reckoned to have taught, we had better believe! But the problem is to discover just what the scriptures really do teach, especially when we are thinking about who, and what, Jesus is.

That is not easy to do. Indeed, I am rather grateful that writing this book will not place me under threat of being racked by the Inquisition nor burned at the stake by some religious authority for heresy. For, though I am struggling to say neither more nor less than the scripture says, it is inevitable that some of my statements will seem to go too far this way or that. It is too much to hope that any theologian could read these lines without somewhere finding himself in stern disagreement with something written here!

The problem is at first sight a simple one – we have established that Jesus has two natures, one human and one divine; that is, he is both Son of Man and Son of God. But now the question must arise – what relationship do those

---

(39) From Documents of the Christian Church; edited by Henry Bettenson; sec.ed.; pg. 51,52; original emphasis; Oxford University Press, London, 1975.

two natures have to each other? How can they subsist [40] together in the one person? How can Jesus be at the same time both God and man? Those questions are easy to ask; but they are immensely difficult to answer without stumbling inadvertently into the ditch of dissidence!

But perhaps I am overly pessimistic. Perhaps the Lord will give me grace to walk a straight path along the line of truth. At least that is my prayer.

Chalcedon did not solve the mystery of how two natures can subsist in one person, but it did protect the church from solutions that were unacceptable or unscriptural. Indeed, it is doubtful if anyone has ever produced an explanation of the manner of Christ's existence that has not echoed one heresy or another. However, the *Definition of Chalcedon* is about as close to an orthodox view of Christ as one can find. At least, it represents one of the few doctrinal statements on which Catholic, Orthodox, and Protestant Christians are generally agreed!

But 1600 years ago Christians were far from accord on their solution to the mystery of how two natures could subsist in one person –

> Everyone agreed that God and man had come together in Christ, but it was impossible to agree as to how this had occurred. Every solution proposed seemed to lead either to dualism, in which God and man came together without actually uniting, or to a hybrid, in which the fusion of God and man produced a

---

(40) The word "subsist" is a technical expression, which here has the meaning of "continuing to exist;" hence it differs from its meaning in popular use: "to exist on the bare necessities of life." Here is an example of this technical use of *subsist* – "The laws of consanguinity have subsisted from the time of Moses until today."

being who was neither one nor the other, but contained elements of both. The former solution safeguarded the distinction of the natures while sacrificing the unity of the person; the latter held up the unity of the person but compromised the separation of the natures. [41]

Chalcedon confronted this problem, and offered, not a *solution*, but a *definition*. That is, the assembled prelates accepted the mystery of the incarnation, and knew that this mystery would always defy explanation. Nonetheless, it was vitally important for the church to define carefully what it believed about Christ, and thus to place a boundary around what was accepted as sound doctrine. Any proposition that stepped outside this boundary could then be denounced at once as heresy.

Perhaps the key word in the Definition is "recognised" – Christ is "recognised in two natures, without confusion, etc."

Chalcedon did not claim to know how the union of the two natures occurred in terms of biology or genetics – such knowledge was in any case beyond human understanding. But the prelates did recognise what scripture affirmed about Christ. They saw from the gospels that Jesus plainly does possess both natures – that he is both God and man – so they sought to define this perfect union in a way that would avoid presenting a false Christ. [42]

The *Definition of Chalcedon* stresses some important tenets –

- Jesus is fully God, but not God only

---

[41] The source of this paragraph is unknown to me, except that it comes from an article in a magazine, whose name I have lost.
[42] *Ibid.*

- Jesus is fully man, but not man only
- nor is he a kind of intermediate being, neither God nor man; rather, he is both God and man united in one person
- therefore he possesses two natures, divine and human, each of which remains separate and complete in itself, yet subsisting in the one being in perfect union and harmony
- the divine nature is eternal, but the human nature was assumed at the incarnation (that is, at the moment of Christ's conception in the Virgin's womb)
- each of these two natures retains the characteristics and functions appropriate to it, and each remains obedient to its own internal laws (thus the human nature can die, but not the divine; the divine nature is omnipresent, but not the human)
- the union of these two natures in one person does not destroy the individuality of each nature; that is, they do not coalesce to form a third kind of nature, but remain distinct from each other, so that both natures subsist in Christ simultaneously
- this does not create in him some sort of split personality, but means only that he maintains within himself the distinctive characteristics of both humanity and deity
- yet he remains one person, with a single consciousness and probably a single will (this is discussed in more detail below)
- so there is no division within Christ, but everywhere he thinks, wills, and acts as one person; he is not a schizophrenic, such that here a man is speaking, but there a god; always it is the one person who speaks and acts

- in Christ, a single person spoke and acted, in perfect conformity to the laws of his being; but the total effect of his words and works leads to the conclusion that he is both man and God.
- this unity within Christ's person is strongly felt by all Christians, so that instinctively they see him as a sole Man, yet one in whom God dwells, who is in fact himself God – *the God-man*.

You might be finding all this tiresomely difficult. But there are two reasons why you should press dauntlessly on. One of them is a little frivolous, the other imperative –

- ***frivolous*** – read on with gratitude, because what you are reading in these pages is (I hope) simpler and clearer than the lengthy and learned tomes I have had to struggle through in order to distil this essence of sound doctrine about Christ!
- ***imperative*** – read on with awe, because your very life depends on just who and what Jesus really is!

As Millard Erickson writes –

> The problem is that man is separated from God by the great gulf of sin. For fellowship between God and man to be reintroduced the gap must be bridged. Someone who is both God and man must bring the two together. If Jesus was not fully God, the bridge does not quite meet at the divine end. If he were not completely man, the bridge does not reach to the human side. The full incarnation is not simply a theoretical

problem of theology – it is a practical necessity upon which man's salvation rests. (43)

If Chalcedon represents *orthodox* belief, what are the *unorthodox* beliefs it is meant to guard us against?

---

(43) <u>The New Evangelical Theology</u>; Marshall, Morgan and Scott; London; 1969; pg. 108; emphasis mine. This book, by the way, is not one of those "tomes" mentioned above!

Chapter Seven

A CLUSTER OF HERESIES

Let us look first at some ancient heresies, and then some modern ones.

ANCIENT HERESIES

THE EBIONITES

Ebionite comes from a Hebrew name meaning "poor", and it was intended to convey the idea of humility, and of suffering for the cause of righteousness.

The Ebionites were Jewish Christians who lived in and around Jerusalem, which they revered as a city made holy by the presence of God. They kept the laws of Moses, used only the gospel of *Matthew*, and rejected Paul as an apostate from the law. They believed that Jesus was the natural son of Joseph and Mary, but because of his special goodness he was elevated to the position of Son of God. This occurred at his baptism, at which time the Spirit of the eternal Christ (who was thought to be higher than an archangel but less than God) descended upon him. After the collapse of the Jewish nation the Ebionites gradually dwindled, until they were swept away in the 7th century by the Muslim conquest of Syria.

Their views were the forerunners of a theory called *Adoptionism*. That is, Jesus was –

> a man who, by a special decree of God, was born of a virgin, and who, after having been thoroughly tested, was given supernatural powers by the Holy Spirit at the time of his baptism. As a reward for his sterling character

and his achievements, he was raised from the dead and adopted into the sphere of Godhead. He was thus a man who became God. (44)

Adoptionists argued that their theory preserved a clear distinction between the two natures of Christ, and that it adequately explained both his human and his divine characteristics. But it hopelessly divided Jesus into two disparate parts. It also reversed the emphasis of the NT, which shows that the motion of the incarnation was from God to man, not man to God.

In other words, the gospel teaches that the eternal Son of God came down and took on human nature, not that the man Jesus of Nazareth reached up and grasped divinity. God became a man; man did not become God (see Jn 1:14; Ro 8:3; Ga 4:4; 1 Ti 3:16; He 2:11-14; 1 Jn 4:2-3).

DOCETISM

Docetism is a name based on the Greek *dokeo* = "to seem." It is known to have been propounded by Cerinthus (circa 90AD), and was thus one of the earliest heresies to affect the church. John was almost certainly arguing against Docetic ideas in *1 John 4:2-3* (see also 5:6; Jn 1:14; etc.).

Docetists held differing views, but all of them contained the idea that in one aspect or another Jesus only "seemed" to be real.

Some held the idea that Jesus was the natural son of Joseph and Mary, and that the Christ-spirit came upon him at his

---

(44) Baker's Dictionary of Theology; editor-in-chief E. F. Harrison; Baker Book House, Grand Rapids, Michigan; 1978; pg. 26. Other information on the Ebionites was gathered from various sources, but mainly The New International Dictionary of the Christian Church; general editor J.D. Douglas; Paternoster Press; 1974. I have used those two dictionaries either as original sources, or to confirm the accuracy, of the whole section on "Ancient Heresies".

baptism, but then left him prior to his crucifixion (a claim based on Jesus' dying words, *"Why have you forsaken me?"*). Others believed that from the very beginning his body was unreal, being only a kind of phantom-form, or an apparition. Still others said that Simon of Cyrene not only carried Jesus' cross, but was actually crucified in his place.

In each of those views either Jesus' real humanity or real divinity was sacrificed – more commonly, his humanity, for Docetism was rooted in an ascetic abhorrence of the flesh, and a reluctance to believe that the holy Son of God could have ever come into any real contact with a human body.

Docetism in its various forms continued to influence the church for several centuries. Muhammad was influenced by Docetism, and this is reflected in the Koran –

> The people boasted,
> 'We have killed Jesus Christ the Son of Mary,
> The Messenger of Allah' –
> But they did not really kill him,
> Nor even crucify him,
> But it was made to appear to them
> As if they had killed him. (Sura 4:157)

> Jesus Christ the Son of Mary
> Was no more than a Messenger of Allah;
> He was the Word of Allah bestowed on Mary;
> He was a Spirit proceeding from Allah. (Sura 4:171)

> Jesus was no more than a Servant
> We bestowed our favour on him,
> And we made him an example
> To the Children of Israel. (Sura 43:59)

ARIANISM

Arianism was more subtle than other heresies, and therefore more dangerous. Fostered by a presbyter in Alexandria called Arius (early fourth century), it taught that "there was (a time) when Christ was not;" that is, that

- the Son of God was created by the Father,
- he was therefore not eternal,
- and thus must be less than the Father.

The controversy provoked by Arius raged for many years, and for some time his followers were the predominant group in the church. But (largely through the determined efforts of another presbyter, Athanasius) orthodox Christology gradually regained its position, and Arianism was defeated. It has, however, continued to arise from time to time, and in our day is most visibly embodied in Jehovah's Witnesses – although Arius, who was largely orthodox in his beliefs, would certainly not have endorsed all the teachings of that sect.

Arius based his argument on the statement that Christ is *"begotten"* of the Father (Jn 1:14,18; 3:16; etc.). He took this to mean that Christ must have had a beginning. But his opponents rejoined that he was wrong to liken a divine begetting to a human begetting. If a man begets a son, it is an act of his will located in time – he can choose whether or not, and when, to become a father. But the begetting of Christ by the Father is an eternal act, located in the very nature and being of God – Father and Son are co-existent and co-eternal.

Arius maintained that Christ, having been begotten by God, became himself the creator of everything else in the universe – beginning with the Holy Spirit, then the angels, then man. Thus Christ is an intermediary being between the Father and the rest of creation.

Because of this unique and exalted station, Christ deserves to be called God, and to be worshipped. Nonetheless, Arians argued that while Christ is very close to God, he is still separate from, and secondary to, the Father.

Other Christians contended that to deny true deity to Christ, while continuing to worship him, was to become idolatrous, thus opening the way to a disastrous resurgence of polytheism.

These matters became the subject of discussion at the Council of Nicea in 325 AD. The argument focussed on two words, with only one letter (in Greek, the letter *iota, ι*) differentiating them. The Arians said that Jesus was "of similar essence" to the Father – Greek, *homoi-ousios*; the others said that he was "of the same essence" – Greek, *homo-ousios*. Ultimately, the Council produced *The Creed of Nicea*, which was modelled on a document presented by Eusebius of Caesarea (it was in fact the creed used in his own church –

THE CREED OF NICEA

We believe in one God the Father All-sovereign, maker of all things visible and invisible;

And in one Lord Jesus Christ, the Son of God, begotten of the Father, only-begotten, that is, of the substance of the Father, God of God, Light of Light, true God of true God, begotten not made, of one substance with the Father, through whom all things were made, things in heaven and things on the earth; who for us men and for our salvation came down and was made flesh, and became man, suffered, and rose on the third day, ascended into the heavens, is coming to judge the living and the dead.

And in the Holy Spirit.

And those that say 'There was when he was not,' and, 'Before he was begotten he was not,' and that, 'He came into being from what-is-not,' or those that allege that the son of God is 'of another

> substance, or essence, or created, or changeable,'

these the Catholic and Apostolic Church anathematises. (45)

It is interesting to note how little this creed says about the Holy Spirit. Discussion of the doctrine of the Spirit had to await a later century.

Notice, too, the unfortunate attitude now beginning to creep into the church – a curse upon those who disagreed! (Arians, after all, were generally zealous and missionary-minded Christians.) But the anathema expressed in the *Creed of Nicea* was mild compared to that contained in a letter the bishops sent to the churches in the same year (325 AD) –

> ... the bishops assembled at Nicea, who constitute the great and holy Synod, send (you) greetings in the Lord... In the first place, examination was made into the impiety and lawlessness of Arius and his followers ... and it was unanimously decided that his impious opinion should be anathematised, together with all the blasphemous sayings and expressions which he has uttered in his blasphemies ... All these utterances the holy Synod anathematised, not enduring the hearings of so impious, or rather so demented,

---

(45)   The more familiar "Nicene Creed" is adapted from this creed.

an opinion, and such blasphemous sayings ... (46)

Orthodox the Synod may have been, but "holy" – or at least gracious – it was not.

APOLLINARIANISM

By the time the dust from the Arian controversy had settled, the true divinity and the true humanity of Christ were firmly established as the orthodox doctrine of the church, and any other view was rejected as heresy. But then arose the problem of how the two natures could successfully combine in one person.

One solution was offered by Apollinarius, Bishop of Laodicea in the late fourth century. He believed that Jesus had a human body, but not a human soul or mind. Thus Christ's human nature was located only in his possession of a body; while his spiritual nature was provided by the Logos (the divine Spirit), which took possession of the body conceived in Mary's womb. Thus the Logos took the place of the rational human soul that all other human beings possess.

This view was condemned, because, while it defended the full deity of Christ, it did so at the cost of his true humanity. He could not be reckoned to be truly a man unless he did possess, not only a human body, but also a human soul, mind, and spirit.

A Council was held in Constantinople in 380/381 AD, to debate the matter, and the following Statement was issued by Archbishop Gregory of Nazianus –

---

(46) The *Creed of Nicea*, and the bishops' letter, are from Bettenson, op.cit., pg. 25,40-41.

THE STATEMENT OF GREGORY

Do not let men deceive themselves and others by saying that ... (Christ) is without a human mind. We do not separate the man from the Deity, no, we assert the dogma of the unity and identity of the Person ... who in these last days has assumed manhood also for our salvation; in his flesh passable, in his Deity impassible; in the body circumscribed, uncircumscribed in the Spirit; at once earthly and heavenly, tangible and intangible, comprehensible and incomprehensible; that by one and the same person, perfect man and perfect God, the whole humanity, fallen through sin, might be created anew.

If anyone has put his trust in (Christ) as a man without a human mind, he is himself devoid of mind and unworthy of salvation. For what he has not assumed he has not healed; it is what is united to his Deity that is saved ... Let them not grudge us our entire salvation, nor endue the Saviour only with the bones and nerves and appearance of humanity. (47)

NESTORIANISM

Nestorius became Bishop of Constantinople in 428. He was a stern opponent of Arianism, and strenuously sought to give equal place to the divine and human natures of Christ. He was also strongly opposed to an epithet that was being commonly applied to the Virgin – *Theotokos* = God-bearer, which he deemed blasphemous. However, in the process of developing his views he created a new heresy, which led to

---

(47)   *Ibid.* pg. 45

his condemnation by a Synod at Rome (430), and his eventual exile to the Great Oasis in Egypt.

Nestorius taught that Jesus was actually a kind of dual personality – one human and one divine – without any real union between them. He insisted that Mary was the mother of the human personality, but not the divine. That is why he refused to accept the designation of Mary as *Theotokos* (God-bearer), but preferred *Christotokos* (Christ-bearer). [48]

The Church agreed that Mary was not the mother of Christ's divinity, but refused to accept *Christotokos* because of its implied dualism. That is, *Christotokos* suggested that Christ's manhood has an existence independent of his divinity.

That in fact was also the weakness of Nestorianism – it inevitably resulted in a denial of any dynamic union between the two natures of Christ. They were left standing side by side, with hardly more to hold them together than a common purpose – rather like husband and wife, who become "one flesh," but remain two separate natures and persons. [49]

---

(48) It is doubtful if anyone in the 5th century church would have accepted the later reading of *theotokos* as "Mother of God." That phrase has (or has been given) connotations that are lacking from the Greek word.

Bettenson says that "God-bearer" conveys the sense of the Greek better than "Mother of God"; for the Greek word "stresses the Deity of the Son rather than the privilege of the mother."

In later Roman Catholic thinking, of course, *Theotokos* did become more vitally associated with Mary than with Christ. It was thought to say more about Mary than it did about Jesus. But that was not the intention of those who first coined the word. They were trying to formulate a Christology, not a Mariology

(49) The latter part of this sentence is from Bettenson, op.cit., pg. 46.

So *Theotokos* was insisted on as the only orthodox way of describing the incarnation. Mary was not the "Christ-bearer," nor the "Man-bearer," but the "God-bearer."

One of the chief opponents of Nestorius was Cyril, Bishop of Alexandria (412-444). He wrote a letter on the matter, which is now called *Cyril's Exposition* –

CYRIL'S EXPOSITION

> ... (The two natures of Christ) which were brought together to form a true unity were different; but out of both is one Christ and one Son. We do not mean that the difference of the natures is annihilated by reason of this union; but rather that the Deity and Manhood, by their inexpressible and inexplicable concurrence into unity, have produced for us the one Lord and Son Jesus Christ ... It was not that an ordinary man was first born of the holy Virgin, and that afterwards the Word descended upon him. (The Word) was united with the flesh in the womb itself ... Thus it is one Christ and Lord that we acknowledge, and as one and the same we worship him; not as a man with the addition of the Word ... because the body of the Lord is not alien from the Lord; and it is with this body that he sits at the Father's right hand. (50)

EUTYCHIANISM

Bettenson succinctly describes Eutyches – "an elderly monk of Constantinople, whose anti-Nestorian zeal far outran his imperceptible theological discretion." He propounded a view that was virtually the opposite of Nestorius. Eutyches taught

---

(50)   Ibid. pg. 47,48

that Jesus' nature was neither human nor divine, but rather a blending of both, a kind of deified humanity. His extreme views on the single nature of Christ eventually led to his condemnation as a heretic, at Chalcedon in 451.

The problem with Eutyches' view lay in his denial that Christ retained a real human nature, which had the result of disqualifying Christ from making any genuine atonement for human sin (if Jesus was not a true "second Adam", then he could not atone for the sins of that first Adam – Ro 5:14; 1 Co 15:22,45,47). Only a righteous *Man* could die for unrighteous *men*.

Prior to his condemnation at Chalcedon, Eutyches wrote to Leo, the Bishop of Rome, hoping to solicit his support. However, Leo decided against Eutyches, and wrote a letter to the patriarch of Constantinople declaring his view on the matter. This letter is known to history as ....

THE TOME OF LEO

> ... God is believed to be both Almighty and Father; it follows that the Son is shown to be co-eternal with him, differing in no respect from the Father. For he was born of God, Almighty of Almighty, co-eternal of eternal; not later in time, not inferior in power, not dissimilar in glory, not divided in essence ... For we could not overcome the author of sin and death, unless he had taken our nature and made it his own ... Thus the properties of each nature and substance were preserved entire, and came together to form one person. Humility was assumed by majesty, weakness by strength, mortality by eternity; and to pay the debt that we had incurred, an inviolable nature was united to a nature that can suffer.
>
> And so, to fulfil the conditions of our healing, the man Jesus Christ, one and the same

> mediator between God and man, was able to die in respect of the one, unable to die in respect of the other ... Thus there was born true God in the entire and perfect nature of true man, complete in his own properties, complete in ours ... Each nature preserves its own characteristics without diminution so that the form of a servant does not detract from the form of God. (51)

The *Tome* was tabled at the Council of Chalcedon in 451, where its balanced teaching became the basis of the famous *Definition* with which I began this chapter. After Chalcedon, the thinking of the Church on the nature of Christ became generally stable. There were other controversies, particularly relating to the Trinity, but Chalcedon finally established that Christ had to be viewed as one person with two natures – human and divine. Thus he is wholly divine and wholly human; both fully Son of Man and fully Son of God.

Notice however, that orthodox Christian doctrine can never do any more than attempt to describe the nature of Christ, as it is portrayed in scripture. To explain or prove the nature of Christ is beyond the reach of human thought.

MODERN HERESIES

I had planned to begin this paragraph with the ancient adage, "There is nothing new under the sun" – the idea being that modern heresies are really no more than echoes of old heresies. That is partly true. Almost all the old heresies have their modern counterparts in the teachings of some sect or group. Even Christians who reckon themselves orthodox can be heard speaking carelessly enough to incur the taint of

---

(51)   *Ibid.* pg. 49,50

heresy – although, fortunately, we are more tolerant now of diverse views than the ancients were!

But we do have to contend today against a set of Christologies that our forefathers never dreamed of encountering; and it was the realisation of this that made me change the wording of my opening paragraph.

The Christologies I am referring to are created by those modern theologians and philosophers who think of the Bible as a collection of myths; who reject the very idea of a miracle; who reckon the orthodox view of Christ is illogical and irrelevant to human need today. These are new heresies indeed, for at least the ancient combatants were agreed in accepting scripture as an inspired revelation of God to man!

But we are now confronted by teachers who want to create their own Christ out of their own rewriting of the Bible. So we have a *mythical* Christ, a *humanist* Christ an *existential* Christ, a *revolutionary* Christ, a *dialectical* Christ, an *evolutionary* Christ, a *political* Christ, and the like. No longer is man made in the image of God; it is now God being forced into an image made by man.

I toyed with the idea of discussing some of these modern Christologies. But then realised there is little that you, my reader and friend, could hope to gain from such a discussion. If you accept that the Bible is an inspired and reliable witness, then these modern theories are blasphemous nonsense (even if they do contain a few valuable insights).

If however you have joined the critics in casting the Bible onto the rubbish dump of hoary legend, then every page of this book must be or you anachronistic flummery.

For my part, I am satisfied that any attempt outside of scripture to explain the marvel and mystery of Christ, must fail. I think I know what Jesus would say to these inventors of new ideas, if they should happen to listen to him –

> *You don't know where I come from, nor where*
> *I am going. You pass judgment on me without*

> *knowing what you are talking about! (Jn 8:14-15)*.

Here are some of the more important scriptural statements about Christ –

SCRIPTURAL STATEMENTS

So far we have seen that the structure of Christ is unique. He is one person; yet in him there are two natures – the divine and the human. There are several passages where this dual nature is mentioned, but always Christ is described as possessing only a single consciousness and will. [52]

JOHN 1:1 FF.

I have already described how this passage declares the Logos to be God. But John also declares that the Logos became *"flesh"* (v. 14). That can only mean he became human; for in scripture the word "flesh" has the basic sense, "physical human nature."

Thus, Eve is described by Adam as *"flesh of my flesh"* (Ge 2:23); humanity is described as *"all flesh"* (Ge 6:12; Ac 2:17); Paul talks of his absence from a certain place as being absent *"in the flesh"* (Cl 2:5); he describes Onesimus as a brother *"in the flesh"* (Phm 16); and so on.

Those references all indicate that the word "flesh," in its basic form, means normal, human physical existence. That is what Christ took upon himself.

Notice how carefully John expresses himself. He does not say that the Logos "came upon", "clothed himself", or even "merged" with flesh; for that would open the way to some

---

(52) This section is adapted from my brother's original notes (see the *Preface* to the companion volume to this one, viz. <u>Emmanuel – Part One</u>).

form of Adoptionism. Rather, he says that the Logos "became" flesh – which compels us to believe that the Logos and humanity were irrevocably joined at the moment of conception in the Virgin's womb. Jesus was one person, with a single will, but two natures, divine and human.

PHILIPPIANS 2:5-11

Jesus was in the "form" of God and was equal with God. The word used by Paul is *morphe*, which always signifies "a form which truly and fully expresses the being that underlies it." In other words, to say that Christ was in the *form* of God is to say that what he appeared to be was what he actually was. The same word is used in the phrase, *"the form of a slave."* Christ did not just appear to be the servant of men, he really was.

The word *schema* is used to describe his human appearance (*"found in human form,"* v. 8). This word emphasises outward human appearance. It suggests here that while Jesus appeared to be a man (and his body was real enough) he still retained beneath that *schema* (human form) his essential divine nature, *morphe* When Jesus was *"transfigured"* before the disciples (Mt 17:2), he revealed something of his original *morphe* or form – the Greek verb is *metamorpheo*, which is based on the noun *morphe* (cp. our English word, metamorphosis).

1 TIMOTHY 3:16

This verse is possibly part of an early Christian hymn. It recognises that the manifestation of Christ is a mystery – that is, it finally lies beyond the realm of human understanding. Yet Christ is a mystery revealed, for he *"appeared"* in a body, and was seen by men and women.

Some manuscripts read, *"He appeared ... ,"* others, *"Who appeared... ,"* others, *"God appeared ...."* In each case the reference must still be to God. If Christ was just a man there would be no point in saying that *"he appeared in a body"*, for he could hardly do anything else! But if he was actually God, then this is worth saying. Logically then, the one who *"appeared"* was God; *therefore* Jesus was both God and man.

HEBREWS 2:5-18

Here we learn the following –

- Jesus was for a little while lower than the angels, which implies that normally he was higher than they (v. 9).
- Jesus tasted death for everyone, yet God alone is capable of taking everyone's responsibility upon himself.
- Jesus destroyed the power of death (v. 14), a task for which only the strength of God could be sufficient.
- Jesus also himself suffered death (v. 9), but while man is susceptible to death, God is not.
- Jesus *"partook"* of our nature (v. 14), which means that he was truly human.
- Jesus was *"made like his brethren in every respect"* (v. 17), so that he might genuinely represent us. No clearer statement of the full humanity of Jesus could be made. Thus this passage teaches both the deity and humanity of Jesus. He is the God-man.

FINAL PROPOSITIONS

Now it is time to put all that we have discovered into the form of propositions that will, hopefully, present the truth, prevent error, and come as close as human words can ever come to defining the mystery of Christ. These propositions may stretch the minds of some of my readers, who may prefer to move on to the delightful quotes that close this chapter. But if you want to grasp an orthodox view of Christ, and come to understand your Saviour as nearly as possible, then ponder this summary –

- In the man Jesus of Nazareth there is but one person, who is the Son of God, the eternal Logos.

- However, while Jesus is only one person, he does possess two natures, one human, and one divine. The divine nature has belonged to the Logos from eternity; the human nature was assumed by the Logos through the incarnation; so that now the Logos possesses both natures in perfect balance with each other.

- The human and divine natures are not fused or merged into each other; they remain distinct and separately distinguishable, but exist within the one person, the Logos, in complete harmony.

- The Logos did not come upon an existing human person, one who had an already existing identity. Rather, he assumed a human nature at the moment of conception in Mary's womb, and at once imparted his personality to that nature (remember there is only one person, not two). The personality of Jesus of Nazareth is that of the Logos.

- Within Jesus there is a single awareness; that is, he does not think of himself now as a man, and now as God, but simply thinks of himself as himself. There is no hint in scripture of a divided consciousness in Christ. There is in him only one self, not two.

- If there are two natures in Christ, are there also two wills? Controversy over this question led to the excommunication (in 681) of a number of church leaders, including a Pope!

Pope Honorius I allowed that Christ possessed "two natures, unmixed, undivided, unchanged, both operating what was characteristic of each;" but he also argued that Christ possessed only one will, that of the Logos. For this he was anathematised by the Council of Constantinople, which insisted that Christ had two wills, human and divine, with the human will ever in voluntary submission to the divine. The issue still remains unresolved.

Many thinkers since the 7th century, including many great modern theologians, have pronounced the Council wrong and the 7th century Pope right on this matter – that is, they reckon that Christ has one will, not two. Others disagree. The argument hinges on the issue of whether a "nature" can exist without its own will. Thus some argue that the human nature of Christ must have a human will, as the divine nature has a divine will. Others contend that the Logos supplied his own will to the human nature he assumed at the time of the incarnation.

What is the correct position? Who knows! It seems a small point on which to excommunicate anyone, let alone a Pope! My feeling is that just as Jesus possessed a single consciousness, so also he possessed a single will. But whether or not that was so in theory, it was certainly true in practice; for if Jesus did possess a separate human will, then it was (and is) totally unified with the will of the Logos. He always appeared to be, and acted as, a person with single, undivided volition.

- The divine nature of Christ remains impassible – that is, incapable of experiencing *inflicted* suffering, that is suffering forced upon him against his own choice to experience it.

The Logos is beyond the power of death, free from ignorance. insusceptible to weakness or temptation. Yet the Son of God still suffered and died, but did so through his human nature – so that the man Jesus of Nazareth died, but the Logos did not (and could not) die. But note that *impassibility* cannot mean (as some claim) that God is void of any emotion or sensibility, for the Bible attributes to him a wide array of sensitivities. He truly *feels* the pains of his people and enters sympathetically into their sufferings (He 4:15; Ho 11:8).

There is however, a mystery here. No one can suppose that any creature can hurt the Creator, unless he chooses to allow that pain. Yet, if he is indeed Love (1 Jn 4:8, 16), how can he *not* respond to the rejection, disobedience, suffering, pain, or sorrows of those he loves? How can he *not* rejoice when those he loves return his love with adoration and devout service? A love that does not love, or that does not behave lovingly, is unworthy of the name. Love is always vulnerable to hurt. Love is always responsive to love. Love cannot do less than act in accordance with its own nature. So, in that sense, God *is* forced into certain responses or actions by human behaviour. Whatever truth lies in the idea of *impassibility* must be modified by such considerations as those.

- The properties of both natures are now the properties of the one person, Christ, so that he can be said to be omnipotent, omniscient, and so on; but also (during the years of his incarnation and still, as the Son of Man, in heaven) to be subject to normal human limitations – such as spatial boundaries, and the like.

However, care must always be taken to avoid suggesting that any human weakness has passed over to the divine nature, or that any uniquely divine property has been communicated to the human nature.

- We are careful to talk about the "union," not the "fusion," of the two natures, noting that Jesus as a man could exercise divine powers only derivatively, and the Logos vice versa. There is an analogy here with the way the soul acts through the body, and the body through the soul; each sharing in the attributes of the other, but without confusion of identity. In practice however, during the years of his incarnation, Jesus drew on no power or resource, save what was available to him as a righteous man limitlessly filled with the Holy Spirit (Jn 3:34).

- The end result of this union of the two natures in one person has been to create a Saviour who is not God-in-man, nor God-and-man, nor man-in-God, but rather God-man.

Now let me conclude this chapter with two sayings from the old divine, Thomas Watson –

> Christ took our flesh that he might make the human nature appear lovely to God, and the divine nature appear lovely to man ... He humbled himself more in lying in the virgin's womb than in hanging upon the cross.

> It was not so much for a man to die, but for God to become man was the wonder of humility ... That man should be made in God's image was a wonder; but that God should be made in man's image is a greater wonder. [53]

---

(53)   A Body Of Divinity; Banner of Truth; 1958; pg. 137.

Chapter Eight

EVER WITH THE FATHER

> So long as we conceive of God only as the Absolute and the Eternal, infinitely remote from man, such a union of God and man is unthinkable; we could as easily imagine a union between a star and a fly. But long before we read of the Incarnation, the Bible teaches us that God is a Person, with thought, and will, and love, and that there is a real kinship between him and man, since man is made in his image. That is to say, there is something corresponding with humanity in God, and something corresponding with divinity in man, so that a union between the two is not inconceivable. [54]

With this chapter we begin a study of the mystery that Christians call the *Incarnation*, and we will do it by looking at four powerful aspects of the person and life of Christ –

- his pre-existence
- his virgin birth
- his kenosis
- his purpose.

---

(54)   C. F. Hunter, <u>What A Christian Believes And Why</u>; Methodist Church, London; 1942(?); pg.67.

THE PRE-EXISTENCE OF CHRIST

Which of the following statements is the most accurate?

- Jesus Christ was a great religious teacher, even a prophet; but he was neither God nor the son of God.
- Jesus Christ was a man, who because of his sinless life and mighty works was made the Son of God.
- Jesus Christ was and is fully man and also fully God.

Even among regular church-goers you might find many who agree with the first statement (although it is hopelessly unscriptural); and you would probably find about the same number who would correctly choose the last statement. But many others would just as readily choose the second. It sounds about "right," and it doesn't throw up too many mysteries or difficulties. Yet you will know by now that it is woefully inadequate as a summary of what scripture says about Jesus.

Why are people, even Christian people, so ill-informed? How can they hold such unsatisfactory ideas about Christ?

One prime reason is failure to grasp the fact of Jesus' pre-existence. The thinking of too many people about Jesus never goes further back than the nativity scene at Bethlehem. But scripture shows that he existed with the Father before the world began.

The first suggestions of a pre-existent Messiah are found in the OT (Ps 2:7; 110:1-2; Is 9:6; Mi 5:2); and the apocryphal *2 Esdras 12:32; 13:26; 14:9*. (55) This concept of a Messiah who

---

(55) "He is the Messiah, whom the Most High has prevented from appearing until the end of the days ... the Most High has held the Messiah in readiness during many ages; through whom he will deliver the world ... To you *(Esdras = Ezra)* I now say (that) you are about to be taken away from the world of men, and then you
(continued on next page)

was already dwelling with the Father in heaven, waiting for the day of his coming to earth, was not strongly developed in Judaism; yet it was there plainly enough, and it provided the base for Jesus' own assertions of his pre-existence, and for the teaching of the apostles.

Jesus gave to the Jews a startling announcement of his pre-existence – *"Truly, truly, I tell you, before Abraham was, I am!"* (Jn 8:58).

Nor did the apostles hesitate to be equally bold in their assertions about Christ – "For you know the grace of our Lord Jesus Christ, that though he was rich (pre-existence), yet for your sake he became poor (incarnation), so that by his poverty you might become rich" (2 Co 8:9). What a remarkable association of ideas! Paul seizes the majestic doctrine of the pre-existence of the Son of God and suddenly links it with the humble theme of Christian charity (vs 1 ff).

Just as Jesus surrendered the wealth he had with the Father from eternity, and came down to earth to be poor among us, so should we be eager, out of the abundance God has given us in Christ, to help one another.

The pre-existence of Christ can best be seen in two relationships – with the Father, and with the Creation *(which I will take up in the next chapter)* –

HIS ETERNAL RELATIONSHIP WITH THE FATHER

CHRIST IS BEGOTTEN BY THE FATHER

– see Jn 1:14,18; 3:16; Ro 8:3; Ga 4:4; Cl 1:15; 1 Jn 4:9.

(continued from previous page)

will abide with my Son along with those who are like you, until the end of time."

The idea behind those verses is that the Logos has always been related to the Father as his Son, and that this relationship springs out of an eternal act of generation by the Father, one that had no beginning and will have no end. If Jesus were not the Son of God then we should have to find another who is, for God cannot be Eternal Father except in conjunction with an Eternal Son. Fatherhood and Sonship begin together, and are dependent upon each other.

Angels are "sons" of God by an act of divine *creation*; Christians are sons of God by an act of divine *adoption*; but Christ is uniquely the Son of God by a perpetual act of divine *generation*. His Sonship no other can emulate. He is the "only" Son of God, not made, but begotten for ever.

Christ is the Only-Begotten of the Father in five ways –

ESSENTIALLY

Christ is the Son of God by virtue of his nature; the essence of deity belongs to him, for he is eternally begotten from the Father (Jn 6:57; 10:30,38; 14:11; 17:21; Cl 1:19). The chief statement of this great mystery is in *John 1:18*, which reads literally –

> *No one has ever seen God; the only-begotten God, who is into the bosom of the Father, he has made him known.*

There are two strange sayings in that verse – "*the only-begotten God*"; [56] and "*into the bosom of the Father*". [57] Both of those statements convey a powerful sense of the complete union of the Son with the Father. All the fulness of God dwells in Christ. He is not placed beside the Father as

---

(56)　The manuscript evidence for this reading (which is shown only as a footnote in the RSV) is strong.

(57)　John uses the strong Greek preposition *eis* = into, instead of the expected weaker preposition *en* = in.

someone other than God, but he penetrates into the very heart of the Father. His endless source is at the very Centre of the Godhead.

The Father begets, has always begotten, and always will beget the Son. Between Father and Son there is a dynamic and perpetual flow of life. How majestic, how glorious, how awesome is this splendid Saviour! How incredible the condescension, the measureless love, that led him to forsake *"the ivory palaces"* and to make his home among the squalor of humanity (Ps 45:8). Oh! the depth of the riches, wisdom, and knowledge of God! (Ro 11:33). Only the crassest mind could contemplate without thrilling awe this gracious revelation that God has given us of his own inner being.

OFFICIALLY

Christ is the Son of God by virtue of his office as Messiah. That is the special sense of Psalm 2:7; Acts 13:33; Hebrews 1:5; 5:5.

Hence it was at the inauguration of Jesus' Messianic ministry that the Father spoke from heaven (echoing the words of the psalmist) – *"This is my Son, my Beloved, with whom I am well pleased!"* (Mt 3:17). The Jews, said Jesus, should not have been offended by his claim of the title "Son of God", for they already knew that this was one of the proper titles of the Messiah. Any man who claimed to be the Messiah necessarily had to be known as Son of God (cp. Mt 26:63; Lu 1:35; Jn 20:31).

So Jesus quite rightly challenged his opponents –

> *(Why) do you say of him whom the Father consecrated and sent into the world, 'You are blaspheming,' because I said, 'I am the Son of God'? (Jn 10:36).*

When the Father spoke from heaven at the time of Jesus' baptism, and echoed the words of the psalmist, he was in effect publicly proclaiming to Israel the Messiahship of Christ.

Later, the same proclamation was made in the presence of Jesus' closest disciples –

> *A bright cloud overshadowed them, and a voice from the cloud said, 'This is my Son, my Beloved, with whom I am well pleased; listen to him!' (Mt 17:5).*

Many years later, Peter was still overwhelmed by that divine encounter, and he struggled for words to describe it –

> *We were eyewitnesses of his majesty. For when he received honour and glory from God the Father and the voice was borne to him by the Majestic Glory ... we heard this voice ... for we were with him on the holy mountain (2 Pe 1:17-18).*

SPIRITUALLY

Christ is the Son of God by virtue of his limitless possession of the Spirit (see Jn 1:32-34; and cp. Mt 3:16; Mk 1:10; Lu 3:22). This possession was indeed *"without measure"* (Jn 3:34); which confirms the love the Father has for him and shows that the Father *"has given all things into his hand"* (v 35).

ETHICALLY

Christ is the Son of God by virtue of his obedience to the Father's will (Jn 4:34; 5:19,30; 8:28; 12:49; 14:10).

This obedience was demanded of him because he was a Son; and then his Sonship was confirmed by the perfection of his obedience – *"Although he was a Son, he learned obedience through what he suffered."* Nor is this merely an interesting idea. On the contrary, it is for us sinners a matter of life and death; for, having been made perfect by his obedience, Christ then became *"the source of eternal salvation to all who obey him"* (He 5:8-9).

The "perfection" wrought in Jesus by his obedience to the Father was not, of course, *moral* perfection. He was never at any point in his life anything less than absolutely impeccable. Upon his moral character there was never the least stain, not so much as a minute blemish. Yet that perfect holiness had to be proved in the crucible of temptation and pain, and only by suffering could he be perfected as the Saviour of his fallen, hurting people (He 2:14-18; 4:14-16).

NOMINALLY

Christ is the Son of God by virtue of raising himself from the dead –

> *This is why the Father loves me – I lay down my life, that I may take it up again. No one takes it from me, but I lay it down of my own free will. I have power to lay it down, and I have power to take it up again. That is the command I have received from my Father (Jn 10:17-18).*

What kind of man can say such things? Who is this who claims that his life is invincible, and that death is powerless before his will? Who can read such words, and accept them, without a tremble of awe in their souls? Many, of course, find them impossible to believe – *"He has a demon, and he is mad; why listen to him?"* (vs 20). But then, how could a madman speak the amazing and beautiful things this Man spoke; and how could a demoniac do such wonderful things? (vs 21).

Jesus could speak thus only because he was totally aware of his identity as Son of God. He knew that death could strike at his human nature and cast it down to the grave; but he also knew that his divine nature, the eternal Logos, was utterly beyond the reach of death. As the undying Word of the

Father, he could call life back into his dead human frame whenever he chose to do so.

So Jesus charged the Jews to recognise this – his resurrection from the grave in which they were planning to bury him would be proof that God was indeed his Father, and that he is truly the eternal Son of God.

Paul too recognised that this was a central fact in the resurrection – "Jesus Christ our Lord was designated Son of God in power according to the Spirit of holiness by his resurrection from the dead" (Ro 1:4). He who is alive from the dead by an act of his own ageless will must be named **Son of God in power**!

But now, the pattern of Sonship exemplified in Christ should be reflected in each one of us who believe in him. As Jesus is *Son* of God essentially, officially, spiritually, ethically, and nominally, so, by pale parallel, are we the *children* of God –

- by ***generation*** – being "born again" or "regenerated" into the Father's family (Jn 1:13; 3:3,5; 2 Co 5:17; Tit 3:5; Ja 1:18; 1 Pe 1:3).

- by ***designation*** – being recipients of an office and title in the church which is the body of Christ on earth, each of us having a place and function in that church appointed for us by God (Ro 12:3-8; 1 Co 12:4-12, 27-28).

- by ***inspiration*** – being temples of the Holy Spirit (1 Co 6:19), who bears witness with our spirits that we are the children of God (1 Jn 2:29; 3:8-10).

- by ***acclamation*** – being promised that the day of our resurrection will as surely proclaim our sonship as Christ was proclaimed Son by his resurrection (Ro 8:18-19; 1 Jn 3:1-3).

CHRIST IS ETERNAL WITH THE FATHER

– see John 1:1-2,18; 17:5,24; Revelation 1:17; 2:8; 3:14; 21:6; 22:13.

He is the *Alpha* and *Omega*, the first and the last, the beginning and the end.

Alpha and *omega* were the first and last letters of the Greek alphabet. In the NT they are linked together to form a proverbial phrase with a fairly wide meaning, containing elements of Hebrew, Greek, and Latin idiom –

- in *Hebrew*, the combination of the first and last letters of the alphabet (*aleph* and *tau*) formed an idiom meaning "the first and the last," or "the beginning and the end."
- in *Greek* and *Latin*, however, the terminal letters of the alphabet formed a phrase more akin to the idea of "completeness" (like the English "everything from A to Z.")

All those ideas lie in the NT use of *"Alpha and Omega"* – "the first and the last, the beginning and the end, the completeness of all things."

Alpha and Omega is used by John both of God and of Christ –

– of God in Revelation 1:8; 21:6

– of Christ in Revelation 22:13

The use of the same expression, in the one book, of both Christ and God is a powerful statement of the equality of Christ with God. Whatever *Alpha* and *Omega* means in relation to God, must also be true of Christ.

What then does it mean, to say that God and/or Christ are *Alpha and Omega*? The expression almost certainly echoes such sayings as –

> *I, the Lord (Yahweh), was there at the beginning, and I will be there at the end. I am the one who from the beginning has decreed how it will all end (Is 41:4).*
>
> *Before me there was no other god, neither shall there be any gods after me (43:10).*
>
> *I am the first and I am the last; apart from me there is no god! (44:6).*
>
> *Hearken to me, O Jacob, and Israel, whom I called! I am he, I am the first, and I am the last (48:12).*

Those sayings comprise an affirmation by God of –

- his eternal nature, without beginning or end
- his uniqueness, for there has never been, nor ever will be, any other god.
- his utter transcendence, higher than anything humans could think
- his majestic greatness, the King of ages, the Sovereign Lord of all time and eternity.

All that and more is collected into the vivid saying, *"I am the Alpha and Omega."* This glory the Father and the Son share equally (cp. also Ro 11:36; Ep 1:10, 22-23).

From the earliest times the appellation *Alpha and Omega* was given to Jesus by Christians everywhere. There are countless inscriptions of those two Greek letters still extant on walls, tombs, monuments – all of them an analogue of Christ, and attesting a belief in his deity.

The *Alpha and Omega* is also frequently applied to Christ in the writings of the Fathers. This use was never disputed in the church, not even by heretics, who were often embarrassed by it, and tried to find some way to escape its evident meaning. But the issue could not be evaded. The universal application of the *Alpha and Omega* to Christ clearly shows the deep-rooted belief of the early church in his eternal nature – that he had always existed with the Father, and always would, and exists now to help his church.

The *Alpha and Omega* is linked with Christ in four ways –

- **_chronological_** – Christ is the beginning of all things, he is the end of all things; the first and the last; in him they had their origin and in him they will come to their appointed end.

- **_ontological_** – Christ differs from the Father in person, office, and relationship; but in all other respects he is all that the Father is, a Being possessing the full essence of Deity. [58] Just as the *"Alpha and Omega"* shows the self-existence of the Father, so it shows also the self-existence of the Son in the Father.

- **_metaphysical_** – just as the *Alpha and Omega* describes the limitless transcendence of God, so it tells the same about Christ, who also is exalted far above all creation (Ep 1:20-21; Ph 2:9-11).

- **_existential_** – just as the *Alpha and Omega* declares the limitless pre-existence and endless continuance of God, so it confirms that Christ *"was in the beginning with God"* and shared the glory of the Father *"before the world was made"* (Jn 1:2; 17:5).

Thus Jesus was *begotten* by the Father, and he is *eternal* with the Father, and also –

CHRIST IS EQUAL WITH THE FATHER

In the beginning was the Word, and the Word was with God, and the Word was God (Jn 1:1).

---

(58) In _office_, the Father is originator, Christ is mediator; in _relationship_, Christ is filial, the Father is paternal.

The expression, the Word was *"with"* God, does not allow the idea that Christ may have been inferior to the Father (as a lowly pauper might be "with" a mighty prince); nor even that Christ was "with" the Father as a companion or associate. The Greek construction conveys the idea of *"face to face,"* meaning "standing at the same level, sharing the same privileges and powers, enjoying intimate communion as equals."

Paul boldly asserts the equality the Son shared with the Father from the beginning (Ph 2:6); and Jesus himself did not hesitate to claim that he and the Father were *"one"* (Jn 10:30). The Jews had no doubt about what that claim meant, for they at once took up stones to kill him *"for blasphemy, because you, being a man, make yourself God"* (v33).

Christ is *"one"* with the Father in <u>substance</u> (possessing with the Father the fulness of God's being); in <u>character</u> (lacking nothing of the holiness and love of God); in <u>will</u> (agreeing with the Father in all things); in <u>power</u> (having equal access with the Father to the omnipotence of God); and in <u>work</u> (co-operating perfectly with the Father in completing their mutual purpose).

CHRIST IS BELOVED BY THE FATHER

"This is my Son, my Beloved!" (Mt 3:17; 17:5).

While we revel in the love God has for us, and in our love for God, and while we are sure that God finds joy in his love for us and in our love for him, we also know that love finds its deepest satisfaction only among peers. A man may deeply love creatures that live on his farm, or in his house, or even wild in the bush; but he cannot love them as he loves his own wife who lies in his bosom, or even as he loves his children, the image of himself. And if a man lived alone, without wife, child, neighbour, or creature, could any kind of pure love ever be awakened in his heart?

If God is love, if it has always been the nature of God to love – and scripture affirms that this is so – then who was the object of that love before the foundations of the universe were laid?

Could love be awakened even in the heart of God, could God have created the world as an expression of his love, if there had not been, throughout eternity, One who was united with the Father, the receiver and reciprocator of the Father's love? Could God know joy in love even equal to the joy we know, if there were not within the Godhead the possibility of love shared between Divine Peers?

One of the chief glories of the doctrine of the Trinity is that it solves this dilemma; for the Three Persons in the Godhead are shown to have been rejoicing for ever in the unhindered flow of their mutual love.

It is the Father's delight to yield all that he is and has to the Son (He 1:2), as it is equally the Son's delight to yield all that he is and has to the Father (1 Co 15:24); and the delight of the Holy Spirit to be the fountain of all loving joys (Ga 5:22-23), which flow within the Godhead and over into the church.

In this same love, we are to love one another.

Chapter Nine

CHRIST AND CREATION

The quest of the ages has been for a principle of unity and continuity that will interpret the universe.

In their pursuit of a unifying principle, philosophers have offered many different solutions to the meaning of life. For some, the true End of Life has been Pleasure. Others have contended that Reality is found only in Beauty. Still others have extolled Virtue, or Patriotism, or Self-discovery. And there are those who have argued that meaning can be found only in Despair, for the End of all that exists is total Extinction.

But Christians insist that God has spoken to mankind in Christ, and Christ must be acclaimed as the one who provides unity, continuity, and purpose for the entire universe.

That idea is set out in three remarkable and parallel passages of scripture – *John 1:1-5; Colossians 1:15-17; Hebrews 1:1-4*. Using the Colossian passage as a base, I have rearranged these passages to show their similar content –

Colossians 1:15-17	**_John 1:1-5_**	**_Hebrews 1:1-4_**
He is the image of the invisible God ...	In the beginning was the Word, and the Word was with God, and the Word was God ...	God in these last days has spoken to us by his Son, who reflects the glory of God, and bears the very stamp of his nature ...

The firstborn of all creation ...	He was in the beginning with God ...	Whom he appointed the heir of all things ...
In him all things were created, in heaven and on earth, visible and invisible ... all things were created through him and for him whether thrones or dominions or principalities or authorities ...	All things were made through him, and without him was not anything made that was made ...	Through him also God created the world ... When he had made purification for sins, he sat down at the right hand of the Majesty on high, having become as much superior to the angels as the name he has obtained is more excellent than theirs ...
He is before all things, and in him all things hold together	In him was life, and the life was the light of men ... the light shines in the darkness, and the darkness has not overcome it.	Upholding the universe by his word of power.

It is clear that the same set of basic ideas about Christ underlies each of those passages, yet the passages are different enough in their contexts and styles to make it improbable that they are copies of each other. It is more likely that their similarity indicates that these basic ideas about Christ were universally believed in the church from its earliest days. In other words, the concepts underlying those three passages did not originate with their authors, but were part of the common faith Christians had in Christ almost from the day of Pentecost.

Some scholars have argued that the church could not have developed such profound ideas so early. But that ignores the verbal teaching of Jesus himself, who said the most astonishing things about his identity with God, and about his universal power; and it also ignores passages in the OT that clearly prepared the way for the NT doctrine of Christ.

One of the most notable of these, is the discourse on Wisdom in *Proverbs 8:1ff*. Wisdom is personified, and said to be pre-existent with God, acting as his agent in creation and in redemption –

> *When he established the heavens I was there ... when he marked out the foundations of the earth, then I was beside him like a master-workman, and I was daily his delight ... He who finds me finds life ... all who hate me love death (vs 27,29,30,35,36).*

Although the Jews did not specifically identify this personified Wisdom with the Messiah, nor think of this Wisdom as the Son of God (except perhaps in an allegorical sense), it was inevitable that Christians should at once read "Christ" for "Wisdom" (cp. vs 17 with Jn 14:21; vs 23 with Jn 17:5; vs 30 with Jn 1:2-3; and 9:2-3 with Jn 6:27).

So, based on the personal teaching of Jesus himself, and the witness of the OT, the early church swiftly developed a magnificent vision of Christ, exalted and glorious, a vision that is all the more stunning when you remember they were talking about a man whom many of them had actually met and touched! (See *1 John 1:1-3*; and also *John 2:22-23; 10:21; 11:45; 12:10-11,42*; which all show, because of the manner in which Jesus spoke, and the mighty works he did, that many people believed what he said about himself, no matter how preposterous his words seemed to be.)

What then was this consensus about Christ that the church so early reached? Essentially it contained two great statements –

> ***Christ is the Creator of all things***
> ***Christ is the Upholder of all things***

CHRIST IS THE CREATOR OF ALL THINGS

That proposition is stated admirably in the three passages set out above, which declare that –

CHRIST IS PRE-EXISTENT TO THE CREATION

Christ was in the beginning with God, he is the image of God, he reflects the glory of God, he bears the very stamp of God's nature, *he is God.*

> *"He who has seen me," said Jesus, "has seen the Father" (Jn 14:9).*

The invisible God has become visible in Christ. He who was with the Father from the beginning, for a time came down to earth. His purpose? To reveal to us in himself the likeness of God. Having done so with consummate grace, he then returned to his proper place at the right hand of the Majesty in heaven.

Yet his appearance defied all natural reason. He did not look like a pre-existent Deity; on the contrary, he looked like an ordinary man! In what sense then did he resemble God? How did he represent God to the eyes of mankind? Could such a thing be even remotely possible? How can even the Almighty find a way to become human?

The answer lies in one of the first and most basic propositions of the Bible – *"mankind is made in the image and likeness of God."*

God is able to express himself in human form because the human image already carries the shape of the divine image. If mankind had not from the beginning been moulded into the likeness of God, the incarnation would have been impossible. Thus the Lord God could not, and would not, incarnate himself into, say, a dog, for that would require him to deny his own nature and decree. Even to take the nature of an angel would be impossible for God, for angels are *not* made in his *"image and likeness"*. But we are!

Thus when Adam was made, he was fashioned in resemblance to the pre-existent Christ and he reflected the glory of Christ. The ravages of sin have not been able completely to deface this stamp of Christ's nature in man. Thus a human form was at least partly familiar to Christ; it was not wholly foreign.

CHRIST HAS PRIMACY OVER THE CREATION

He is the first-born of all creation (Cl 1:15).

Scripture does not mean that Christ is the *first* creature made by God; he is not the *"first-created"* but the *"first-born."*

The expression *"firstborn"* was a Hebrew idiom that meant "having pre-eminence," or "holding the highest position." Paul himself is careful to clarify his meaning in the next verse – Christ could not be himself created, for *"in him all things were created, in heaven and on earth, visible and invisible"* (vs 16).

The idiomatic use of the expression "first-born" can be seen in *Psalm 89:27*, referring to King David: *"I will make him the first-born, the highest of the kings of the earth"* – there "the first-born" of the kings means simply "the highest" of the kings. So the pre-existent One is also the pre-eminent One, and the entire creation lies inescapably under his rule.

CHRIST IS THE PURPOSE OF THE CREATION

Four prepositions are used of Christ in relation to the created universe

- *"all things were created **in** him"* – he is the Word of the Father, the source of universal power.
- *"all things were created **through** him"* – he is the Agent of the Father, who does nothing except through and by the Son.
- *"all things were created **for** him"* – he is the Goal of the Father, the appointed heir of all that has been made.
- *"**without** him was not anything made that was made"* – he is the Companion of the Father, the centre of the Father's counsel, the sharer of the Father's will.

All things gain their existence from Christ, and in him all things will find their eventual consummation. He is *"the beginning and the end ... the first and the last."*

It is worth noting that Paul, who says everything exists *"in, through, and for Christ,"* elsewhere makes a nearly identical statement about God the Father: *"For from him, and through him and to him are all things. To him be glory for ever, Amen"* (Ro 11:36). It is hard to see how Paul could have spoken about both God and Christ in such equal terms, unless he was persuaded that Christ and God share equally the same divine nature.

CHRIST IS THE PROGENITOR OF THE CREATION

One of the problems faced by the early church was caused by a group of false teachers who argued that Christ was only one of a series of angelic or divine beings. They claimed it was not possible to approach God directly through Christ, but the assistance of these other spiritual intermediaries was also required.

The letter to the Colossians was written primarily to counteract this false teaching (which later developed into a heresy called "Gnosticism").

Paul scorned the very idea that we needed any intermediary between ourselves and the Father except Christ; and he was even more disdainful of the suggestion that various grades of angels could act in this capacity. Paul insisted that _all_ angels, without exception, were created through Christ and for him; and the apostle to the Hebrews declared that Christ, both in his name and nature, is superior to even the highest angel (Cl 1:16; He 1:4).

The idea behind such passages is that

- Angels have no power apart from Christ. In fact, apart from him they cannot even exist. They are 'creatures,' nothing more. To the salvation of men and women they, by themselves, can contribute nothing. They can only _"render service"_ (He 1:14), and this always in subjection to Christ and through his power.

- The "good" angels cannot add anything to the fulness of riches and resources that believers have in Christ. The 'evil' angels cannot separate them from his love (Ro 8:35- 39).

- In fact, through his death these sinister powers were vanquished (Cl 2:15). They are approaching the day when their ability to do harm in God's universe and in the hearts and lives of earth-dwellers will be ended once and for all (1 Co 15:24,25). [59]

---

(59) Hendriksen, op.cit., _Colossians_, in loc.

CHRIST IS THE UPHOLDER OF ALL THINGS

> *He is before all things, and in him all things hold together ... He upholds all things by the word of his power ... in him is life, and his life is the light of men. (Cl 1:17; He 1:3; Jn 1:4)*

How awesome to contemplate the limitless immensity of the power that Christ is reckoned to wield, a power that is exercised by nothing more than his will as expressed by his word. He speaks, and it is done. Should he withdraw that word for a moment, all life would instantly cease. The world was made from nothing by the word of Christ; and by a syllable it can be turned back to nothing (He 11:6).

No wonder Paul is able to say that a mere touch of his "breath" will be sufficient to annihilate Antichrist and his hordes (2 Th 2:8). As easily as a man might change a garment, so Christ will one day roll away the present heavens and earth and replace them with a new heaven and a new earth (He 1:10-12; and see also 2 Pe 3:12-13; Is 65:17; Re 21:1).

In the meantime, all that exists, does so by his will. From him comes all life and all light. The darkness wars against that light, but cannot overcome it, for the very darkness itself could not continue except by his permission:

> *I am the Lord, and there is no other. I form light and create darkness, I build prosperity and I wreak havoc. I am the Lord, and I do all these things ... I am the Lord, and there is no other, beside me there is no God. Although you don't know me, still I will strengthen you ... and will call you by your name, and entitle you woth great honour. (Is 45:4-7)*

Now it requires faith to look out across the earth and to declare that the nations all find sustenance and coherence in Christ. Disorder often seems more apparent than order. The shrieks of the tortured, the moans of the dying, the tears of the bereft, seem to indicate divine neglect rather than divine control. Chaos seems a more likely end than Paradise. But that is a surface view. The larger story of human life is love, not hate; it is purpose, not futility; there have been more years of peace than of war, more kindness than cruelty, more laughter than tears.

But why *should* that have been so unless it is true that Christ names and governs even those who are not aware that he exists? And even when he allows darkness to engulf the earth from time to time, there is still no defiance of his purpose. In the end, all things serve him, as they also serve those who especially belong to him (Ps 30:1; Pr 16:7; Ro 8:28).

If all things are Christ's, then all things are mine in Christ. No evil can really befall me (Ps 91:10), because what my enemy meant for evil becomes in Christ turned to my good (cp. Ge 50:20). Every happening in my life can be turned by faith into an upward step on the pathway to Paradise.

No wonder Paul could write:

> *All things are yours, whether the world, or life, or death, or the present, or the future, all are yours; and you are Christ's; and Christ is God's (1 Co 3:21-23).*

Chapter Ten

BORN OF A WOMAN

Now we come to the mystery of the *incarnation* of Christ. He who was with the Father from the beginning, he who has neither beginning nor end, is yet said to have had a beginning – when he was born in Bethlehem of Judea to Mary, his virgin mother.

Is that truly possible? Can a woman who has not lain with a man conceive and give birth to a son? Is the virgin birth of Christ sober history or pious myth? On that question Malcolm Muggeridge writes –

> ... Mary, in delivering Incarnate God into the dangerous world, has to be, at once, the most radiant and warm-blooded of mothers whose breasts gush with milk, and a virgin untouched by any sensual hand or carnal experience. The Holy Child has come, fleshly, out of her flesh, and, at the same time, not through fleshly processes. As she proclaims in her 'Magnificat,' God has regarded her lowliness, and made her blessed in the eyes of future generations, by bestowing upon her the inestimable privilege that in her womb the Incarnate happens ... (However) in humanistic times like ours, a contemporary virgin – assuming there are any such – would regard a message from the Angel Gabriel that she might expect to give birth to a son to be called the Son of the Highest as ill-tidings of great sorrow and a slur on the local family-planning centre. As a matter of fact, under existing conditions it is extremely improbable that Jesus would have been permitted to be born at all.

Mary's pregnancy, in poor circumstances, and with the father unknown, would have been an obvious case for an abortion; and her talk of having conceived as a result of the intervention of the Holy Ghost would have pointed to the need for psychiatric treatment, and made the case for terminating her pregnancy even stronger. Thus our generation, needing a Saviour more, perhaps, than any that has ever existed, would be too humane to allow one to be born ... Are we, then, to suppose that our forebears who believed implicitly in the Virgin Birth were gullible fools, whereas we, who would no more believe in such notions than we would that the world is flat, have put aside childish things and become mature? ...

It would be difficult to support such a proposition in the light of the almost inconceivable credulity of today's brain-washed public, who so readily believe absurdities in advertisements and in statistical and sociological prognostications before which an African witch-doctor would recoil in derision. (60)

Thus with caustic perception Malcolm Muggeridge writes about the virgin birth in his brilliant essay, *Jesus – The Man Who Lives*. He goes on to stress the unhappy fact that, in modern society, people who believe in a miraculous happening like the virgin birth are reckoned imbeciles; but to "disbelieve in an unproven and unprovable scientific proposition like the Theory of Evolution," or, still more, to question any other "quasi-scientific shibboleth ... is to stand

---

(60)   Malcolm Muggeridge, op.cit., pg. 23-27.

condemned as an obscurantist, an enemy of progress and enlightenment."

Well, whether or not some think we are fools, we boldly confirm our faith that "when the time had fully come, God sent forth his Son, born of a woman, born under the law, to redeem those who were under the law so that we might receive adoption as sons" (Ga 4:4-5). So, in response to the gospels, and in the words of the creeds, we believe that this Son of God was supernaturally conceived in the womb of his virgin mother, Mary.

THE GOSPELS

See *Matthew 1:1-25*, which tells the story of Jesus' birth from the viewpoint of his step-father, Joseph. Matthew also places special emphasis upon Joseph's Davidic lineage, which would have been legally conveyed to Jesus upon Joseph's death. Note that Joseph was in direct line of descent from the ruling family in the House of David (through the line of Solomon) – thus Jesus' throne-pedigree (that is, his legal right to succeed to David's throne) is established (cp. also Ac 2:30; 13:23; Ro 1:3; 2 Ti 2:8; etc).

See *Luke 1:26-2:20* and *3:23-38*, which tell the story of Jesus' birth from the viewpoint of his virgin-mother, Mary. Unlike Matthew, who emphasises Christ's royal lineage, Luke, by taking the genealogy of Jesus right back to Adam, stresses his affinity with the entire human family.

From earliest times, the apparent discrepancies between the genealogies given by Matthew and Luke have been explained by supposing that Luke actually gives Mary's genealogy (not Joseph's). If that is so, then Mary's genealogy was also Davidic, but through the family of Nathan (not Solomon). Thus Luke, like Matthew, may be showing Jesus' physical link with the royal family, except that he traces it through Mary, while Matthew does so through Joseph.

THE CREEDS

<u>The Apostle's Creed</u> says –

> I believe ... in Jesus Christ his only Son our Lord: Who was conceived by the Holy Ghost, born of the Virgin Mary ...

<u>The Nicene Creed</u> says –

> ... Who for us men and for our salvation came down from heaven, And was incarnate by the Holy Ghost of the Virgin Mary, And was made man...

What is stated in the gospels and the creeds was certainly the universal faith of the early church, although some critics have argued that the nativity "legend" was a later accretion to the gospel.

From the mass of patristic evidence available, let two passages from Ignatius (c. 110) suffice. They stress the importance given to the virgin birth in early Christian belief –

> Under the Divine dispensation, Jesus Christ our God was conceived by Mary of the seed of David and of the Spirit of God; he was born, and he submitted to baptism, so that by his Passion he might sanctify water ... Mary's virginity was hidden from the prince of this world; so was her child-bearing, and so was the death of the Lord. All these three trumpet-tongued secrets were brought to pass in the deep silence of God. How then were they made known to the world? Up in the heavens a star gleamed out, more brilliant than all the rest; no words could describe its lustre, and the strangeness of it left men bewildered ... The age-old empire of evil was overthrown, for God

was now appearing in human form to bring in a new order, even life without end. (61)

Glory to Jesus Christ, the Divine One who has gifted you with such wisdom ... You hold the firmest convictions about our Lord; believing him to be truly of David's line in his manhood, yet Son of God by the Divine will and power; truly born of a Virgin; baptised by John for his fulfilling of all righteousness; and in the days of Pontius Pilate ... truly pierced by nails in his human flesh ... so that by his resurrection he might set up a beacon for all time to call together his saints ... (62)

The fact is, if the virgin birth of Jesus is denied, then grave questions are raised about the validity of every part of the gospel, for there can be no serious doubt that the nativity stories were an integral part of the original gospel – both in its earliest oral form, and in the later written versions of *Matthew* and *Luke*.

Mark and *John* make no specific mention of the virgin birth, but it is clearly assumed by both writers, as it is everywhere in the NT. Critical objections have been raised against the virgin birth, but they have all been satisfactorily answered many times. I want to concentrate here on the story itself, and on its value for us.

---

(61) *Letter to the Ephesians*, 18,19; tr by M. Staniforth, op.cit., pg. 81. The translator adds this note: "The notion that the devil was completely hoodwinked by the secrecy of the Incarnation became a favourite in early theology."

(62) *Letter to Smyrna*; *ibid*; pg. 119. Notice how Ignatius includes the virgin birth among a simple statement of the bedrock truths of our faith, and he was a contemporary of the apostle John, and may even have known Jesus.

THE NATIVITY STORY

Latourette beautifully summarises the story of Jesus –

> Born in a manger in Bethlehem, the town associated with the name of David, the most glamorous of the Jewish kings, and reared in the village of Nazareth, Jesus grew up in a humble family. From the hills back of Nazareth a commanding view could be had of the plain of Esdraelon, crammed with history, and of snowy Hermon. From what we know of his later years, we may be fairly certain that Jesus often climbed these hills and, always sensitive and observing, fed his soul on the beauty around and below him and thought deeply on the life unrolled before him ...
>
> That the household was deeply religious is borne out by many bits of evidence – the accounts of the conception and the birth of Jesus (in *Luke*), much of which could only have come from his mother Mary; the other narrative of his birth (in *Matthew*), which was presumably, at least in part, from Joseph, his reputed father; the delicacy, beauty, and deep religious feeling of the nativity stories ... careful compliance with the Jewish law in circumcision and in the ceremony of consecrating Jesus to God in the temple, as Mary's first-born ... the custom of Mary and Joseph to go every year ... to Jerusalem to the feast of the Passover.
>
> We are not surprised that Jesus formed the habit of going to the synagogue, that he learned to read, that his chief reading was in the sacred books of his people, and that, even at the age of twelve, he meditated profoundly on the issues raised by them. Since, after Jesus began his

public career, we hear no mention of Joseph as living, we may assume that he had died and that Jesus had been left to earn the living for his mother and his younger brothers and sisters. (63) It is, indeed, conceivable that the delay in entering upon his itinerant ministry was due to his feeling of responsibility for shelter and daily food for the dependent members of the family. (64)

DEFINITION OF THE "VIRGIN" BIRTH

Precisely what is meant by the concept of a "virgin" birth? I have suggested earlier that the phrase is partly misleading. The birth of Jesus was not a miracle of *parturition*, but rather of *conception*. He was supernaturally *conceived*, but otherwise his gestation and birth were quite normal. This is well expressed in the following –

> The virgin birth of Jesus, as presented in the Bible, was a birth in normal human flesh from a normal human mother who was a virgin in the strictest sense of the word. That is, not only did Jesus have no human father, but no coitus

---

(63) See Mt 12:46-47; 13:55; Mk 3:31-32 (which in some Gk mss includes the word "sisters"); 6:3; Lu 8:19-20; Jn 2:12; 7:3,5; Ac 1:14; 1 Co 9:5; Ga 1:19. Opinion is divided as to whether these "brothers and sisters" were *(1)* cousins of Jesus; *(2)* the children of Joseph by an earlier marriage; *(3)* children Mary bore to Joseph after the birth of Jesus. Apart from a pious reluctance to think of Mary as anything other than a virgin, there seems to be no real reason to deny the natural reading of the various passages, namely, these people were uterine brothers and sisters of Jesus. (But for the Catholic view on this matter, see *Addendum*.)

(64) A History of Christianity, Vol 1; Harper & Row, New York, 1975; pgs. 35-36.

of any kind, natural or supernatural took place. (65)

It is vital to realise that Mary's virginity was not disturbed by the divine *"overshadowing"* (Lu 1:35), for this is what places the nativity story into a unique category. There is no parallel in any other literature or religious tradition. Jesus was not a man born of human parents, who become apotheosised after his birth, in the manner of the ancient Greek heroes. Nor was he a kind of half-god, half-man hybrid, born out of a weird sexual union between a god and a woman. (66) Such ideas were common in the pagan world, and in the ancient myths; but there is nothing in them anywhere that resembles the purity and sheer beauty of the story of Mary and her Infant.

Nor would the condescension of the gospel have been comprehensible to the ancients. They could imagine a god having some kind of liaison with a woman, and thus conceiving a strange child. But it never entered their heads to tell about the god *himself* humbly submitting to the confines of the womb and of human birth!

Compare the gospel with the following stories.

---

(65) Baker, op.cit., pg. 543,544.

(66) As, for example, Zeus is supposed to have done in various camouflages. Such as when he disguised himself as a swan in order to approach slyly and then seduce Leda, the daughter of King Thestius. The beautiful Helen of Troy was born of this gross union.

Chapter Eleven

PERSEUS and ASCLEPIUS

The ancient Greeks told numerous stories about gods having intercourse with women, whose offspring became the heroes of the famous myths. Sometimes these heroes were half-divine when they were born; at other times they underwent a part or full apotheosis either during their life-time or after death.

THE MYTH OF PERSEUS

Perseus was one of the greatest of the Argive heroes. He is most renowned for slaying the terrible Medusa. This is the story of his birth.

King Acrisius of Argos had no sons, but he was favoured with a most beautiful and virgin daughter, Danae. The king loved his daughter, but he yearned also for a son, and resolved to ask the oracle how he could procure a male heir. He was told: "No son will be yours; yet your grandson will slay you!"

Moved by fear, he ordered that a prison of brass be built, and that his daughter Danae should be incarcerated there for the rest of her life. So it was done. The heavy brass door was firmly locked, and guarded day and night by savage dogs.

But the supreme god Zeus looked upon the lovely girl in her sorrow, and he came down upon Danae in a shower of gold, and lay with her in her cell. She bore him a son, whom she called Perseus. When Acrisius heard of this, he refused to believe that the child was a son of Zeus, but was convinced that his own brother Proetus had seduced Danae. However, since he could not bring himself to kill his own daughter, he took her and the baby and locked them in a wooden box, which he cast into the sea, thus giving them into the providence of heaven.

The tiny ark was eventually washed up onto the shores of an island, Seriphos, where it was opened by a fisherman who took Danae and Perseus to King Polydectes, the lord of the island. Polydectes welcomed them into his palace, and reared Perseus as though he were his own son ... (the myth then continues through many astonishing adventures, until finally, by accident, Perseus fulfils the oracle by killing his grandfather with an errant discus.)

THE MYTH OF ASCLEPIUS

A beautiful Greek maiden Coronis often used to sit by the lakeside washing her feet. One day the divine Apollo, the son of Zeus, saw her sitting thus. He loved her instantly, and resolved to possess her as his own. So he became her constant lover. However, a time came when he had to travel to Delphi on business. Being doubtful of the maiden's fidelity, he conjured up a raven with pure white plumage to guard her while he was absent.

But Coronis, although she had yielded to the embraces of Apollo, and was already with child by him, was really in love with Ischys, a handsome Arcadian. So she invited Ischys to take advantage of the absence of her divine paramour, and to come and share the joys of her bed, which he did with gladness

The raven observed their tryst and at once flew off to report the betrayal to Apollo. With great fury he slew the maiden. Preparations were made for her funeral, and a splendid pyre was built. Meanwhile the goddess Diana, who was jealous of Apollo, placed a curse on the raven for its evil report and turned it pitch black. That is why to this day ravens are still the colour of coal.

When the flames began to reach toward the body of the princess, who was still carrying the baby in her womb, Apollo, regretting his hasty anger, rescued the child and gave him to a goat to nurture. The boy's name was Asclepius, and when he reached manhood he was found to possess remarkable healing skills. His fame spread far and wide, and it was said that under his hands no sickness was incurable. Then a day came when Asclepius brought a dead man back to life. Alarm spread across Mt Olympus, the abode of the gods. Mighty Zeus, fearful that humans might learn how to escape death altogether, cast a thunderbolt onto the earth and killed Asclepius. But his father Apollo pleaded for mercy with such fervour that the gods relented, and Asclepius was carried up to heaven and took his place among the stars.

Now that he was divine, Asclepius soon became the Greek god of healing, and his fame began to spread even more widely than it had while he was still human. Temples in his honour sprang up all over the land, and his worship began to spread to other lands. In the year 293 B.C., when their city was suffering from a terrible plague, even the proud Romans sent an embassy to Greece to beg the aid of their healing god. It is said that Asclepius himself came to the rescue of the city, accompanied by a great serpent. When the ship anchored in the Tiber the serpent slithered from it and took possession of a nearby island, upon which a temple was later built to the praise of Asclepius, whose art stemmed the plague and restored health to the Romans. Asclepius took a snake as his attribute because it renewed its skin each year and so provided a sign of his renovative powers. He also carried a sacred staff, around which a serpent is often shown coiled. To this day the staff and entwined serpent remain a symbol for the practice of medicine.

In the time of the apostles the cult of Asclepius, the god of healing, was immensely popular throughout the Greek and Roman world. The ruins of many splendid temples erected for his worship can still be found scattered across the former Roman territories. He was called in the Greek tongue "Soter" – "Saviour", the same title the apostles gave to Jesus. And the benefit people hoped that Asclepius would confer upon them was called "soteria" – "salvation/healing"; again, the word is the same as the one used in the NT. There is something breathtaking about the boldness of the apostles, who plucked the beautiful title *Saviour* right out of the hand of Asclepius and gave it instead to Jesus! They were announcing to the world that what people had hoped in vain, across many centuries, to find from a god who had never existed and could not possibly answer their prayers, was now available in reality from Christ. (67)

But we must return to our main point, which is this – the licentious and sensual elements of such pagan myths are completely lacking from the gospel accounts of the conception and birth of Jesus. Yet it is difficult to explain the absence of such mythology from the gospels, for in those days such additions might actually have made the stories more credible, especially among the lower classes. If the gospels were nothing more than fiction, then the writers, hoping to reach a wide market in the gentile world, would have been under a powerful cultural imperative to include many such fabulous inventions. Instead, of course, the gospels are sober accounts of what the apostles actually saw, heard, and knew to be fact. There is nothing fictitious about them, and there really is no other sensible way to describe them.

INFANCY LEGENDS

What the gospel authors might have written about the conception and birth of Jesus, if they had been free to write out of their own imaginations, is suggested by the many infancy legends that began to circulate among the churches even before the death of the last of the apostles. The fictional early stories about Jesus are filled with fantastic inventions. Miracles, prodigious wonders, amazing signs, abound. Free play is given to curiosity, and many intimate details are revealed, sometimes morbid, sometimes almost prurient.

It was my original intention to include selections from these legends, so that you could contrast them with the calm and pure accounts given in *Matthew* and *Luke*. But after reading

---

(67) There are other slightly different versions of the Asclepius myth, but they all agree on the main thrust of the story.

through a number of them, I have decided that the task of creating a reasonable précis would serve little useful purpose. [68] If you are interested, you will find these legends in any reasonably complete collection of NT apocryphal writings. They are sometimes grouped under the heading, "Infancy Gospels."

Two questions are raised –

- How can the similarities between the nativity story and the Greek myths be explained?

(Note: parallel legends can also be found in Egyptian, Indian, and Persian mythology.)

While the gospel accounts are lacking many elements of the old fables, there do remain some similarities. One major example is the story of the Virgin Birth. Long before the time of Christ, the ancient world had become familiar with the idea of a virgin woman giving birth to a child conceived in her womb by a god, and to the idea of this child being a source of healing and of resurrection to the human race.

Does this mean that the gospels are only an improved version of those myths?

Hardly. Educated Greeks and Romans were already aware that their myths were just that: *mythical*. Intelligent people did not really believe that Apollo had copulated with Coronis to produce the Saviour, Asclepius. So there was little chance that the apostles could add credibility to the gospel by inventing a virgin birth. In fact the claim of a virgin birth was as much a scandal among educated sceptics then as it is now (cp. Jn 9:29).

---

(68) You will find some comments on these matters, along with a number of references, in *Chapter One* of the companion volume to this book – <u>Emmanuel–Part One.</u>

At the time of Christ's birth, even in Athens (where gods abounded) it would have been difficult enough to claim that one of them had caused a virgin woman to conceive. But can you imagine how immeasurably more difficult it was for such a story to be accepted in that bastion of monotheism, *Jerusalem*?

It is perhaps possible to imagine a Greek philosopher trying to convince his hearers that the old pagan myths were true, and that the same events were being repeated in their time. But it is quite impossible to imagine a group of devout Jews doing so.

The very idea of Yahweh becoming flesh through the womb of a virgin woman would have seemed utterly blasphemous to them – unless, of course, it actually did happen. In the face of undeniable fact, despite all their former teaching and prejudice, they were compelled to believe it.

That is why the implicit character of the gospel nativity stories is one of simple truth, told by eyewitnesses. There are abundant signs that we are not reading fiction, but fact. (69)

The best way to explain the similarities between the myths and the gospel, is to recognise that the former indicate –

- **_a universal desire_**, which has been in the heart of man since the dawn of time, for a Deliverer to appear on earth and to solve the awful mystery of human weakness and death (cp. Hg 2:7, AV; Ro 8:19,22-23).

---

(69) I am aware of the various arguments that critics raise against the story of the Virgin Birth, but (as I have already stated) I think they have been satisfactorily answered. It is not possible to examine here either the arguments against the virgin birth, or the evidences for it. Various commentaries, Bible dictionaries, theologies, and the like, can provide you with a full study of these matters.

This immemorial longing has provoked countless fables, oracles, and prayers, many of which contained a glimmering perception of how heaven would finally respond.

- **_a kind of prophetic instinct_** placed by the Holy Spirit within the spiritual consciousness of men and women, to prepare the way for the Christ who would finally make all the dreams, the signs, the oracles, come true.

This intimation of what was to be was first given to Adam and Eve in the garden (Ge 3:15), and it was most clearly maintained among the Hebrew people – but it never quite vanished from the other branches of the human family. The great Hope remained, to be repeated in a thousand different ways, that one day _he_ would come who would set mankind free from pain and mortality.

It has often been pointed out that throughout the civilised world at the time of Christ's birth there was an intense feeling that the time _had_ come, and that the Deliverer would soon appear. Jews, Romans, and Greeks alike shared this expectation (or rather, anticipation) of a Saviour, although each in their own way.

They hated Jesus, not because they did not want a Messiah, but because he was nothing like the mighty warrior king of their legends.

On this matter of a universal premonition of a Saviour, C.S. Lewis writes –

> And what did God do? First of all he left us a conscience, the sense of right and wrong: and all through history there have been people trying (some of them very hard) to obey it. None of them ever quite succeeded. Secondly, he sent the human race what I call good dreams: I mean those queer stories scattered all through the heathen religions about a god who dies and comes to life again, and, by his

death, has somehow given new life to men ... (70)

In my mind the perplexing multiplicity of 'religions' began to sort itself out ... The question was no longer to find the one simply true religion among a thousand religions simply false. It was rather, 'Where has religion reached its true maturity? Where, if anywhere, have the hints of Paganism been fulfilled?' ... Paganism had been only the childhood of religion, or only a prophetic dream. Where was the full grown? Or where was the awakening?

... I was by now too experienced in literary criticism to regard the gospels as myths. They had not the mythical taste ... if ever a myth had become fact, had been incarnated, it would be just like this. And nothing else in all literature was just like this. Myths were like it in one way. Histories were like it in another. But nothing was simply like it. And no person was like the person it depicted ... numinous, lit by a light from beyond the world ... Here and here only in all time the myth must have become fact; the Word, flesh; God, man. This is not a 'religion', nor a 'philosophy'. It is the summing up and actuality of them all. (71)

On the same theme Michael Christensen writes –

Scattered throughout human history are archetypal patterns, stories, rituals, and religious motifs (that parallel the gospel story)

---

(70) Mere Christianity; Fontana Books, London; 1956; pg.. 51.
(71) Surprised By Joy; Fontana Books, London; 1975; pg. 187-189.

> ... How are Christians to understand the obvious similarities between pagan myths and Christianity?
>
> Either pagan mythology is essentially demonic and functions as counterfeit revelation for the purpose of confining mankind, or else it is the dim foreshadowing of God's supreme revelation in Christ ... The archetypal pattern of redemption – birth, death, new life – is 'a thing written all over the world.' (72)

So in Christ the shadowy dreams became reality; the blurred oracles found their sharp focus; the vague premonitions gained amazing substance; the songs, prayers, longings of every human society throughout history found their point of joyful fulfilment.

- **_Why do the nativity stories in Matthew and Luke differ so strikingly_** from the ancient myths, and from the later Christian legends about the birth and infancy of Jesus?

The answer to that question has already been suggested: the former are *factual*; the latter are *fictional*. Had Matthew and Luke invented the virgin birth, their stories would have resembled either the ancient myths, or the foolish fables that *were* invented during the second century about Mary, and about the nativity and infancy of Jesus.

If the gospel stories are fictitious, then they comprise a literary miracle that itself would demand explanation. If the stories were invented, why did the authors omit from them so many things that we would all like to know about Mary

---

(72)   C.S. Lewis, <u>On Scripture</u>; Hodder and Stoughton; London; 1980; pg. 74

and Joseph, and about the childhood of Jesus – things later writers did not hesitate to invent? (73)

The only way to explain satisfactorily the fragmentary nature of the nativity accounts in *Matthew* and *Luke*, and the considerable differences in those accounts, is to accept that the two authors refused to write more than they had been told by reliable witnesses. They recorded only what they had been able to confirm, so they had no doubt about the truth of

---

(73)　For example –

- Mary's father was a very rich man, named Joachim; her mother was Anna; and she was born to them supernaturally after an angel visited them.
- six months after Mary was born she was able to walk unaided.
- at three years of age she was taken to the Temple where she lived until her betrothal to Joseph, and during this time she was miraculously fed by an angel.
- that Mary's hymen remained unbroken after the birth of Jesus, so that she was still a physical virgin; and that a woman who doubted this, and wished to examine her manually, was grievously afflicted by God in her hands, which burned like fire.
- the infant Christ miraculously purified muddy water; fashioned twelve sparrows from a soft clay and then made them fly away; cursed his enemies and made them suffer many things, but blessed and healed his friends.
- while he was not yet six years of age, Jesus raised another child from death, miraculously gathered up water spilled from a broken pitcher, and performed many other such prodigies.
- water in which the infant Christ was washed brought healing to a leprous girl; the ox and the ass in the stable bowed before him and worshipped him; when his parents took him to Egypt, and they were threatened by dragons, lions, and leopards, the baby walked and talked and compelled the wild animals to worship him; he commanded tall palm trees to bend down and yield their fruit to Mary; and so on, through many other bizarre and fantastic incidents.

what they wrote. They refused to indulge in speculation, and were content to tell the story simply, without magical embellishments.

Chapter Twelve

OVERSHADOWED BY THE SPIRIT

There is an even more important reason for rejecting the idea that the gospel narratives are as fictitious as some of the absurd later productions. At the time the gospels of *Matthew* and *Luke* were written *there was no recognised need for Christ to be given a supernatural origin.*

This is plainly shown by the complete lack of direct references to the virgin birth anywhere else in the NT. The NT letters, and the *Acts*, concentrate on the teaching and miracles of Jesus, and especially on his death and resurrection. The virgin birth was not a prominent part of the preaching of the early church. Not until a century or more later, when the church began to grapple seriously with the question of Jesus' identity as the God-man, and how such a phenomenon could have occurred, was it realised that a virgin birth for the Saviour was imperative.

Yet the nativity stories are as old as the gospel itself, for they were in circulation in oral form many years before Matthew and Luke decided to write down the life of Jesus. But why should such a tradition have developed so early, when there was no apparent need for it, unless it was based on ungarnished history, and therefore could not be denied?

So we can read the lovely narratives of Jesus' conception and birth with grateful joy, knowing that in the poetry and charm of these stories there is an awesome revelation of God, a revelation that is the very basis for all our hope of salvation and of eternal life.

THE SUPERNATURAL CONCEPTION

Nowhere is the delicate beauty, the discretion, of the gospel story, better seen than in Luke's restrained account of the meeting between Gabriel and Mary, when the angel said, *"The Holy Spirit will come upon you, and the power of the Most High will overshadow you; therefore the child to be born to you will be called holy – the Son of God."* (1:35)

The dignity of those words reflects an event that was

- **_Physically miraculous_** – for this was not a "virgin" birth of the sort that history has occasionally reported, but rather a supernatural conceiving, unique in human experience; never before witnessed, and never to occur again. It was God preparing a body for Christ by direct creation within the Virgin's womb (He 10:5).

- **_Morally discreet_** – for although a young woman conceives outside of wedlock, we cannot feel that the story is immoral. Here was no passion except the love of God, no pride except the glory of God, no ambition except the service of God, no praise except the worship of God, and no gain except the Kingdom of God!

- **_Spiritually mysterious_** – for we cannot know the nature of this divine *"overshadowing"*. The idea is like that in the opening verses of the Bible, where at the beginning of all things the Holy Spirit *"brooded over the surface of the water."* Thus both the old and the new creations were inaugurated by the Spirit of God, and inbreathed with the essence of heaven.

- **_Theologically profound_** – for as Paul cried – *"great is the mystery of our religion, that Christ came to us in human form."* (1 Ti 3:16) Endless ages will be insufficient to explore the heights and depths of this secret. Indeed, it is a mistake to try to penetrate it too deeply. We must learn to accommodate mystery. Too much knowledge may sometimes be as perilous as too little! (cp. Ro 16:19; Cl 2:18; 2 Ti 3:8). The most brilliant thinkers, at their best, in matters such as these can never advance beyond *"peering through a dark glass;"* they can never go further than *"seeing in part, knowing in part."* (1 Co 13:9,12).

- **_Poetically beautiful_** – for the gospel story is far, far removed in its serene loveliness from the fantasies of both the pagan myths and the inventions of some early Christian writers.

So indeed, there is nothing parallel to this event in any other sacred writing, nor in the traditions and myths of the past. Incarnations of gods, male and female deities copulating with humans, and other wonders, abound. But the manner of Christ's birth, and the very concept underlying it, is unique.

If the gospel story is fiction, then it is the most astonishing invention in all literature. But that is impossible to believe. Remember that the pagan fables (which sceptics say inspired the gospel story) would have been deeply abhorrent to the early Christians, they were all monotheists, worshipping a single holy God. The fables, however, were jammed with squabbling, greedy, and licentious deities, for whom neither vice nor trickery was forbidden.

It is inconceivable that those first Jewish believers would deliberately ape a literary form so repugnant to them. But despite some surface similarities, they knew that the beautiful story of the birth of Jesus was deeply different from the pagan myths. They also knew it was true. And they wrote what they knew, neither more nor less.

So there is no hint in the gospel narrative of the fornication and duplicity that were endemic in the fables. This is not a god coming down in human form and sharing coitus with a woman. (74) Mary was a virgin before she was overshadowed by the Most High, and she was still a virgin after the Holy One had been conceived in her.

The Holy Spirit *"came upon"* her, but he was not the father of her child. In effect, Jesus of Nazareth had no new father. He was already the pre-existent Son by eternal generation from the Heavenly Father. His conception in the womb was not a sexual act, but a creative one that must be understood in a wholly spiritual (not sensual) sense. The Logos was miraculously caused to become incarnate by an act of the full Godhead, including the Son himself.

But we walk on holy ground, and I tremble lest I say more than is reverent.

Across that holy mystery scripture draws a veil. We may not seek to know more than is revealed. The story cannot be told more convincingly, more spiritually, than it has been told by the inspired writers. Read *Matthew*. Read *Luke*. And rejoice in the precious good news they so beautifully tell under the guidance of the Holy Spirit.

THE ANNUNCIATION

It is impossible for me, a man, to reflect on the fact that Jesus was born of a woman, without then being compelled to look on Mary, and upon all womankind, with awe and affection, and with respect and wonder. I cannot do other than echo the angel's salutation, *"Hail, O favoured one, the Lord is with you! Blessed are you among women!"* (Lu 1:28). Mary indeed is blessed, as through her are all of her kind.

---

(74) Remember again the myth mentioned above, telling how Zeus is supposed to have disguised himself as a swan in order to seduce Leda, the daughter of King Thestius.

Whenever I think of the Lord of glory lying curled in the dark confines of a young woman's womb, I look at my own wife and marvel – then I ask the Lord whether I am rendering her the devotion that she so manifestly deserves. If you, Lord, have chosen to so honour woman, how can I do otherwise? (Cp. 1 Ti 2:15, *"she shall be saved/honoured by the birth of the Child"*; and 1 Pe 3:7; Ep 5:25). God has poured such honour upon womankind through Christ, that any true man must shrink with loathing from treating her, especially a good woman, with indifference, derision, injustice, or brutality.

Yet there have been times when the more highly *Mary* has been exalted, the less real honour has been given to her *sisters*. As a consequence of lifting Mary into heaven, she has sometimes been removed so far from the company of other women, that *she* could be revered while *they* have been reviled.

But see how Matthew and Luke, in their careful genealogies, lock Mary firmly into the human family. She herself truly said, *"All generations will call me blessed"* (Lu 1:48); yet in the end, no man or woman can honour Mary any better than they honour the women among whom they live.

Because of Christ, then, Mary deserves to be highly honoured; but so also do all those virtuous daughters who *"rejoice in God as Saviour"* (vs 46-48, 50).

Ponder this also. Luke, who so tenderly and reverently gave us the story of Mary and her Infant, also carefully recorded a later incident –

> *A woman in the crowd raised her voice and said to him, 'Blessed is the womb that bore you and the breasts that you sucked.' But he said,*

'Blessed rather are those who hear the word of God and keep it!' (11:27-28). (75)

THE VALUE OF THE DOCTRINE

A number of important benefits rise out of the doctrine of the virgin birth of Christ. Here is a summary of some of them –

- In view of what has already been discussed in your previous chapters (about the dual nature of Christ) it seems that for him a virgin birth was essential. Luke, for example, tells us that Jesus would be called the Son of God just because of the nature of his birth (1:34).

- In the process of ordinary conception and birth a completely new "person" is created, one who has never existed before, whose consciousness begins in his or her mother's womb. But the personal consciousness of Jesus was eternal. It was not created in the Virgin's womb, but came into it at the instant of conception.

- Christ's human nature alone (not his Person) was newly created in the womb, and then, by a causative act of God, instantly united with the eternal Logos. Thus the divine was allied with the human, and our state was elevated to the throne of God. Conversely, those who ignore, despise, or for some reason have no knowledge of this fusion, must suffer the more dire distress when the Day of Judgment irrevocably reveals the truth.

- The virgin birth made possible the sinless nature of Christ. Mary was told that her child would be "holy," that is, without sin (Lu 1:34). It is impossible to

---

(75) For the Catholic view on Mary, see *Addendum*.

suggest how this was so, for scripture is silent on the matter. Perhaps Christ could have become sinlessly incarnate on earth by another method. But God chose the one revealed in scripture; and, however it was accomplished, the virgin birth *was* instrumental in producing a sinless Child. (76)

- The virgin birth created a break in the continuity of the Adamic line, thus marking the beginning of God's *"new creation"* (2 Co 5:17; and many others). A corollary of this is the termination of the old law of sin, helplessness, and despair (Ro 7:17-25). Until Christ was born, that old law had held the entire race in its tyranny. It ran wild over all men with none to check it. Then Jesus came, over whom sin had no power, and who pronounced both the end of the old enslavement (8:15-16; 2 Ti 1:7) and the beginning of a new era.

- The virgin birth explains as nothing else can how Christ was able to become a true man without inheriting the dark fate that has held all humanity in bondage – <u>death</u>. Because death had no right over him he was able to choose to die, and in so doing, deliver us forever from death's grip (He 2:9, 14-15).

---

(76) It has been suggested that an ordinary baby receives its blood from its father and not its mother, and that sin lies in the blood. Thus Christ, having no human father, and receiving his blood directly from the Divine seed, was born without sin.

That theory must be rejected *(a)* on medical grounds: for, like all other characteristics in the fetus, its blood comes from both parents; *(b)* theological grounds: it is naive to suppose that sin is located in a man's bloodstream – it is located rather in his corrupted intentions. "Christ was sinless," says Barry Chant, "not because he had a certain blood group, but because the Holy Spirit conceived him in holiness!" (op.cit.)

- Without the virgin birth, a completely new act of creation would have been required. That is, a "new" Adam altogether, made afresh from the dust of the earth. But that would have left an uncrossable hiatus between Saviour and sinner; it would have signalled that God was going to obliterate the original race of man, and begin again. To be our Saviour, *"he had to be made like his brethren in every respect"* (He 2:16-17) – which meant that he had to be, like us, in direct line of descent from Adam.

- The virgin birth achieved that miracle. In one stroke it united Christ with the fallen race, yet at the same time enabled him to remain *"holy, blameless, unstained, separated from sinners,"* and thus our true Redeemer (He 7:26).

- Thus, for us, who were fallen and in despair, the happiest day in all history dawned on that first Christmas morning –

> This is the month, and this the happy morn,
> Wherein the Son of Heav'n's eternal King,
> Of wedded maid and virgin mother born,
> Our great redemption from above did bring;
> For so the holy sages once did sing,
> That he our deadly forfeit should release,
> And with his Father work us a perpetual peace. [77]

---

(77) John Milton, On the Morning of Christ's Nativity. (1629)

Chapter Thirteen

ABASED AND EXALTED

We have been looking at the meaning of the great mystery that Christians call the "Incarnation" of Christ. Our search has so far taken us into the glory of his *pre-existence* and the wonder of his *virgin birth*. But *how* could the pre-existent One become born of a woman. How can God become man? How much of the *divine* remained in the *human*? And why was such an extraordinary act necessary?

The answers to those questions will take us up to heaven and back to earth again, as in this chapter we explore the staggering love shown in the profound mystery of how God was able to assume human form in the person of Jesus, live among us, die, rise again, and then return to heaven's measureless splendour.

The glory that Christ eternally shares with the Father defies all power of human imagination. I struggle with words as I try to capture even a glimpse of that radiant majesty. John saw him for a moment, *"his face like the sun shining in full strength,"* and at once fell at his feet like a dead man (Re 1:16-17).

Perhaps the infinite beauty, the blazing deity of the glorified Christ is too much for any human eye to behold at the present time. Perhaps the human mind, this side of the resurrection, is quite unable to capture that alien and exalted Image. One day, of course, we shall be given eyes able to look on him with surpassing joy, and without flinching. But today, a full vision of the supernal majesty of Christ would shatter our poor faculties.

However, since we are his children, a shadowy glimmer of his beauty has been revealed to us (1 Co 13:12). Yet still, because even this dark reflection of his loveliness is so entrancing, we are constrained to wonder if it really ever will be possible for us to gaze safely upon his unveiled lustre? Perhaps it is foolish to imagine that we could ever stand happily in the presence of such dazzling glory?

Indeed, we could hardly believe in such a miracle, except Jesus himself has promised that in the rapture we shall be transformed, to become like him, shining more brightly than the sun (Mt 13:43).

John put it in different words. He claimed that we shall indeed be able to stand face to face with Christ, without being stricken down, because *"when he appears we shall be like him, for we shall see him as he is"* (1 Jn 3:1-3).

But though we are filled with wonder as we contemplate the *eternal* honour of Christ, our amazement must be ever greater when we ponder his *earthly* dolour. What condescension he showed, what humiliation he suffered, when he who was immeasurably rich became poor for our sake (2 Co 8:9).

> So poor was he that he was constantly borrowing – a place for his birth (and what a place!), a house to sleep in, a boat to preach from, an animal to ride on, a room in which to institute the Lord's Supper, and finally a tomb to be buried in. [78]

THE "KENOSIS" OF CHRIST

The most powerful statement of this condescending grace of Christ is found in *Philippians 2:5-11*, a passage that describes Jesus' seven-fold descent into the deepest humiliation, and then his seven-fold ascent into the highest honour –

---

[78] Hendriksen, op.cit., *Philippians*, pg. 108.

> *He was in the form of God, but did not count equality with God a thing to be grasped.*

On the contrary, he descended into humiliation by –

- emptying himself
- taking the form of a servant
- being born in the likeness of men
- being found in human form
- humbling himself
- being obedient unto death
- dying on the cross.

But for this very reason, he has ascended again to the pinnacle of honour, for –

- God has highly exalted him
- and bestowed on him the loftiest name
- that at his name every knee should bow
- in heaven
- on earth
- and under the earth
- and every tongue will confess that Jesus Christ is Lord, to the glory of God the Father.

The technical name for the process by which Christ came from heaven to earth, to dwell among men, is *kenosis*, based on a Greek word used by Paul – *"(Christ) <u>emptied</u> himself."* (Ph 2:7). What was this *kenosis*, this self-emptying, of Christ, that brought him from heaven's loftiest throne to earth's lowest horror? Paul says that

> *although Christ was in the form of God, he did not count equality with God a thing to be grasped, but emptied himself (Ph 2:6-7).*

What does it mean, *he was in the form of God*? What was his *equality* with God? How did he *empty* himself, and of what?

Those are difficult questions to answer while avoiding heresy on this side or that. The church has never been able to agree fully about the meaning of Christ's *kenosis*. For example, a hundred years ago two famous scholars expressed their opinions – (79)

- Canon Gore –

    There is room, no doubt, for much variety of opinion ... and in any case the wise interpreter will be very shy of erecting a 'kenosis doctrine' on a phrase the exact limits of which no man can fix with precise accuracy.

- Professor A.B. Bruce –

    ... the diversity of opinion prevailing among interpreters in regard to the meaning of (this) passage ... is enough to fill the student with despair and to afflict him with intellectual paralysis.

I am bound to say that a century later the scene is no better! In an effort to arrive at some kind of consensus on the *kenosis* I have spent countless hours labouring through various commentaries, lexicons, grammars, biblical dictionaries, and theologies; but I have completed my toils feeling rather like Omar Khayyam – (80)

> Myself when young did eagerly frequent
> Doctor and Saint, and heard great argument
> About it and about – but evermore
> Came out by the same door as in I went!

But that is too cynical. Despite the many uncertainties there is still much wisdom to be found. Perhaps my next few pages will put you in the way to discover it.

---

(79) Quoted by Dr E.H. Gifford, in <u>The Incarnation</u>; Longmans, Green & Co., London, 1911; pg. 3,4.

(80) Edward Fitzgerald translation, *Quatrain 27*.

VARIOUS ALTERNATIVES

Paul claims that Christ *emptied himself* – but of what? and how? Did he empty himself of the *form* of God, or of his *equality* with God, or of both, or of neither?

- Some commentators choose to remain agnostic in the face of such questions.

They argue that Paul did not write, "he emptied himself of it;" but merely, *"he emptied himself,"* without any mention of what was "emptied". He tells us only the *manner* in which Christ accomplished his *kenosis* (by the 7-fold descent), and then the inevitable outcome (the 7-fold ascent). He does not tell us the inner mystery of the *kenosis*.

- Paul's emphasis is not so much on what Christ *abandoned* as it is on what Christ *assumed* – that is, Jesus took on human likeness, and the form of a servant, and became obedient to death.

  The kenosis has generally been taken to refer not to the *subtraction* of divinity, but to the *addition* of humanity. (John Gerstner)

- So (it is argued), we cannot hope to guess what scripture does not plainly tell us about the *kenosis*. We cannot presume to say how many of his divine attributes Christ may have abandoned, or in what way he did so. Nor can we tell how, or by how much, he surrendered his position of equality with God.

We can do no more than describe what it meant for Christ to be *"in the form of a servant,"* to live on earth as a man, to die on a pain-wracked cross. The inner counsels and processes of the Godhead must forever remain mysterious to us. We have to be content with the description given in the four gospels of the outer processes of the incarnation – a description that deals with observable fact, not hypothetical mysteries.

- Those arguments are attractive. There is undoubtedly a strong element of truth in them.

They benefit by clearing away a lot of weary speculation, leaving the soul free to concentrate on the main thing – Paul's breathtaking vision of the transcendent Lord joyfully grasping servitude among men, and providing for us an ineffable example of humble love. Yet most thinkers are reluctant to stop at that point.

- There is within the church an insistent urge to penetrate the mystery of the incarnation as far as thought and scripture will allow. And the fact is, scripture and thought both provide more insight into the *kenosis* than the above arguments are willing to allow.

FIVE SOLUTIONS

Solutions to the mystery of the kenosis fall into five groups –

- *the Logos* gave up all of his divine attributes, and thus, during the years of his incarnation, ceased all cosmic functions, and lost all divine consciousness.

That is, his powers became strictly human, his activities were absolutely earthbound, and he had no personal awareness beyond that of being an adult man – except that he knew from scripture, and by revelation of the Holy Spirit, that he was the one whose coming had been foretold by the prophets.

- *the Logos* gave up the incommunicable attributes of God (such as omnipotence, omnipresence, omniscience), but not the relational attributes (such as love, holiness, truth).

- *The Logos*, since he cannot be separated from God without sundering the deity (which would be absurd) must have remained fully in the heavenlies and in constant possession and use of all his divine powers, while at the same time he was incarnate in Jesus of Nazareth, who as a man had possession and use only of human attributes.

- <u>the Logos</u> surrendered to the Father all control over the exercise of his divine powers, and had no access to them except as the Father himself allowed (which seems to be confirmed by such passages as *Matthew 26:53*, for if Jesus still commanded the attributes of God why could he not call upon the angels himself, instead of asking the Father to send them?)

- <u>the Logos</u> retained all his attributes and powers, but voluntarily refrained from using any of them in such a way as would have disturbed his claim to be a true man living within the confines of human nature (which seems to be confirmed by such scriptures as *Matthew 4:3*, where Satan takes it for granted that Jesus, as the Son of God, could himself turn stones into bread).

The *first* of those solutions is rejected on the ground that Christ, as the eternal Logos, could not altogether put aside his divine attributes without ceasing to be divine, which would have negated his ability to make reconciliation between God and man. The *second* and the *third* are rejected on virtually the same ground – the Logos cannot discard any of his attributes without in the process destroying his divinity. The *fourth* is rejected because it seems to contradict certain statements in the gospels. The *fifth* is rejected on the ground that it is impossible to conceive how Jesus of Nazareth could embrace in human form such divine qualities as the possession of all knowledge, or being everywhere at the same time.

So we are left with a mystery (1 Ti 3:16) that defies any final solution. We find ourselves obliged to echo scriptures, making statements in one place that seem to contradict what we say in another – because there we are talking about the *Man of Galilee*, while here we are talking about the *Son of*

God. How those two natures (the human and the divine) can blend into one person must baffle penetration by any finite mind.

Nonetheless, some things can be affirmed. Among them is the proposition that whether or not he actually retained the independent use of any or all the divine attributes of the Logos, the man Jesus of Nazareth never once stepped outside the boundaries of his human nature. All that he said and did during the 33 years of his incarnation was done as a man, calling only upon those resources that are available to all believing Spirit-filled people. Thus he was able genuinely to set us an example that we can follow – that is, as he did, so we too can we live, in union with the Father by faith, full of the Holy Spirit, and obedient to the Word and will of God (1 Pe 2:21).

Chapter Fourteen

A MAGNIFICENT HYMN

Anyone attempting to interpret *Philippians 2:5-8* (the seven-fold descent and the seven-fold ascent of Christ) should be cautioned by two things –

First, commentators are universally agreed that these verses were originally a poem or a hymn. No one knows who composed it, or why. Was it written to celebrate the glory of Christ, or to say something about our salvation? We cannot tell. But no one doubts that we are reading some lines of poetry. Which means that they cannot fairly be treated as though they were a piece of formal prose. There is a lyrical aspect to poetry that takes words outside of their merely lexical meanings.

Second, Paul did not mention the *kenosis* as part of a serious argument about the nature of Christ, but rather for a very practical reason (vs 3-5). He is drawing upon the conduct of Christ to show how we too should behave. Indeed, there is a sense of extraordinary daring in his use of the mystery of the *kenosis* to enforce such a mundane charge as Christians caring for each other! Nonetheless, his real theme was not the incarnation and exaltation of Christ, but a rebuke of selfishness and conceit; hence it is possible that he did not choose his words with particular care.

So, to express it more technically, Paul's purpose was not theological, nor even christological, but *ethical*.

I do not mean that Paul was careless, but only that extraordinary weight cannot reasonably be put on words that may not have been intended to bear it.

So the comments that follow will endeavour to give a satisfactory account of the *kenosis*, but you will be wise to remember that I am discussing, not a carefully constructed and formal argument, but the words of a poem that was used to provide a fervent plea for the Philippians to be like Christ.

IN THE FORM OF GOD

Christ, being (from the beginning) in the form of God ... (vs 6, lit).

The structure of the Greek text indicates not only that Christ *was* in the form of God, but that he *is*, always *has* been, and always *will* be in the form of God. The verb (which is a present participle) has the sense of a continuous and unbroken state or condition – " ... *being always* ... " So, from the eternal past into the eternal future Christ possesses the "form" of God. That is a clear statement of his pre-existence and of his deity.

The Greek word for "form" is *morphe* = the essential character of a thing; that which cannot be changed without changing the nature of the thing itself. To say that Christ is in the "form" of God does not mean that he "resembles" God (as *we* might be said to do, Ge 1:26-27), but that he possesses everything that is essential to God; he does not merely simulate the Divine, he *is* Divine.

We might say in English that a piece of plastic has been shaped and coloured so that it takes the "form" of a log of wood; yet it only has the appearance of wood, it is not really wood. But a Greek would say that it cannot have the "form" of wood, for if it did, it would actually be wood.

There are some things whose *morphe* can be changed, so that they actually become something else. For example – the *morphe* of water can be changed so that it ceases to be a liquid, and becomes instead two separate gases, hydrogen and oxygen. Or, the *morphe* of wood can be changed by burning, so that it turns into ashes and vapour.

Possibly the *morphe* of everything in creation could be changed, so that everything could become something quite different – with one exception – *the Creator*. He alone cannot change. The form of God is immutable. He has always been, and always will be, the same (Ps 102:26-28; Mal 3:6; He 13:8); his essential nature and being cannot be altered in any way.

It follows from this that Christ, if he does possess the divine *morphe*, must always have been, and always will be, in the form of God, without interruption, and without change. We humans may reflect the *"image and likeness"* of God, but the eternal Logos possesses *the very nature and substance of God*.

If that is the proper meaning of "form," why then did Paul add the apparent tautology, " ... *did not count equality with God a thing to be grasped"*? He did so because, although *"being in the form of God"* and *"being equal with God"* may at first sight appear to be the same thing, there is in fact an important difference.

The setting in which Paul places those words makes it clear he is using "form" to describe the actual nature of God (which is unchangeable), and "equal" to describe the manner, or method, or state in which God chooses to reveal himself (which is changeable). Christ cannot divest himself of the "form" of God, but he can (and did) divest himself of this "equality" with God.

Paul describes this act of divestment by the phrase –

HE EMPTIED HIMSELF

> *He did not count equality with God a thing to be grasped, but emptied himself, taking the form of a servant, being born in the likeness of men (vs 6,7).*

A better translation of the first part of Paul's statement would be – *"Christ did not count continuance in a state of equality with God as a prize to be held at all costs."* The idea is – the magnificent splendour of his position in the Godhead was not a stolen possession, it was not a prize he had seized and must now defend at all costs; on the contrary, it was his right to appear in the glory of the Deity. But far from clinging tenaciously to all the pomp and splendour of his glorious position, he was willing to humble himself, and to dwell in poverty on earth.

In all history, he was the only Man truly entitled to assert his rights – yet for our sake he declined to do so.

However, it is important to realise that Christ set aside only his *position*, not his *powers*. He did not change one form of being for another, but only one state for another. He surrendered the status he was entitled to as God; but he could not have surrendered his divine attributes without ceasing to be God.

If a man is born to be king, he may decline to sit on his throne and to exercise his royal prerogatives, but he cannot alter the fact that he is a prince.

Or, a king already reigning may decide for a time to forsake the pomp and glitter of the court, and to visit his poorer subjects incognito. For a time he may put aside the outward circumstances of his sovereignty, and change a state of wealth for a state of poverty, but he still retains all his royal rights and powers. His mode of living may change, but not his actual being. He remains the king.

So Christ had "equality" with God. That is, the "quality" of his existence with the Father before his incarnation was one of limitless riches and splendour. He dwelt in those visible conditions of glory and majesty which are the ordinary manner of divine existence, but are not essential to it. Christ could lay aside that equality of conditions and circumstances without disturbing his real deity.

That is what he did when he accepted the incarnation; and it was to this condition of surpassing glory he prayed the Father would soon restore him (Jn 17:5).

At this point, certain questions become inevitable –

HOW COULD THE MAN JESUS RETAIN THE "FORM" OF GOD?

Here again, as in other matters relating to the mystery of the incarnation, the church can do little more than state the fact, and be content to accept it. It is easier to say what we *don't* believe than to explain what we *do* believe!

Nonetheless, we are bound to insist, whatever else may be said about the *kenosis*, that Jesus of Nazareth somehow retained the form of God. "Even when the Logos became what he was not (truly man), he remained what he was (truly God)." That has been the confession of the church since the days of the apostles, and to depart from it is to depart from orthodox belief.

Perhaps the following points will help you to see why this is so —

- If Christ is the pre-existent Son of God, eternally begotten by the Father, born unceasingly out of the life of the Father, then it is impossible that there should ever be any interruption of this act of eternal generation.

There can be no discontinuance of the mutual dependence, each upon the other, of Father and Son, nor of the unity of essence and being shared by each. If such a severance could occur there would at once either be two Gods instead of one, or the Father or the Son would suffer loss of deity — but that is absurd. See also *John 10:30*.

- The doctrine of the immutability of God precludes the Logos from undergoing any fundamental change in his nature or in his being.

God cannot cease from being God. If Jesus was one with God before the incarnation, and if he is one with God now, then he was just as certainly one with God during the incarnation.

- Jesus was able to say to Philip, *"He who has seen me has seen the Father,"* only because he knew that the very ground of his being was eternally in the Father and that the life flowing in him had its perpetual source from the Father. Thus he was able fully to represent God to man.

If the underlying form of Christ was not the form of God, then we have no proof that in Jesus of Nazareth the Father was directly revealed. On the other hand, the continuance of Christ in the form of God assures us that the attributes of God, and especially the moral attributes, are faithfully represented in Christ.

Thus the tender compassion of Jesus and his fierce anger, his patient endurance and his urgent demands, his self-sacrifice and his personal assertion, all reveal God's own nature and disposition. Although he did not in any of his words or works step beyond the bounds of what is proper for human nature, neither were any of his words or works such as would be improper for God.

Lacking the form of God, Jesus of Nazareth would have been merely a fine example of what a good man filled with the Holy Spirit can do. Possessing the form of God, he is also a direct revelation of the character of God, with power to reveal God personally to all who come to him.

- Our very salvation depends upon divinity and humanity both being fully present at Calvary –

  Even in the midst of death he had to be the Mighty God, in order by his death to conquer death. (Lensky)

  The union of the two natures in one person is necessary to constitute Jesus Christ as a proper mediator between man and God. His two-fold nature gives him fellowship with both parties, since it involves an equal dignity with God, and at the same time a perfect sympathy with man (He 2:17,18; 4:15,16).

This two-fold nature, moreover enables him to present to both God and man proper terms for reconciliation — being man, he can make atonement for man; being God, his atonement has infinite value — while both his divinity and his humanity combine to move the hearts of offenders and constrain them to submission and love (1 Ti 2:5; He 7:25). [81]

HOW COULD THE MAN JESUS EXERCISE THE ATTRIBUTES OF GOD?

If Jesus had a human mind, how could he have used the omniscience of God, or have been really aware of his deity? Surely no finite mind could contain the infinite wisdom and knowledge of God? Surely any consciousness of personal deity would shatter the sanity of a human mind?

If Jesus had a genuinely human body, how did he retain the attribute of omnipotence; how did he continue to be omnipresent? Surely, before he could accept the confines of human existence, he had no choice but to surrender all those infinite attributes of God, which are so inconsonant with a human form?

I am sure that the answer to such questions really lies beyond the grasp of even the greatest human mind. However, theologians are not noted for timidity, and they have not hesitated to cross even this sacred thane! The daring solutions they offer are astonishing in the sweep of thought they require. Among those ideas are the following —

- It is suggested that the divine Logos, although incarnate in Jesus of Nazareth, was certainly not localised within that human form, but was able to maintain his cosmic functions in union with the

---

(81) A.H. Strong, Systematic Theology; Pickering and Inglis, London, 1958; pg. 698.

Father. Thus he continued to *"uphold the universe by his word of power"* (He 1:3), even while asleep in the Virgin's womb.

- The Logos, when acting in and through Jesus of Nazareth, was content to function within the limitations of human nature (the *kenosis* was a surrender of divine *functions*, not of divine *attributes*); but that same Logos at the same time was also acting outside of the man Jesus, as the eternal and unchanging Word of the Father. In that heavenly action, of course, he continued in the full use of every divine attribute.

- Thus heaven was not actually deprived of the Second Person of the Godhead during the incarnation.

The mystery here is akin to that which occurs in every Christian, for of us it is said, *"Christ is in you, the hope of glory"* (Cl 1:27); yet at the same time the same Christ is seated at *"the right hand of the Majesty on high"* (He 1:3). Strong describes it thus – [82]

> The whole of Christ can be present in every believer as fully as if that believer were the only one to receive his fulness, and the whole Logos can be united to and present in the man Christ Jesus, while at the same time he fills and governs the universe.
>
> By virtue of this omnipresence, therefore, the whole Logos can suffer on earth, while yet the whole Logos reigns in heaven. The Logos outside of Christ has the perpetual consciousness of his Godhead, while yet the Logos, as

---

[82]   *Ibid*. pg. 704.

united to humanity in Christ, is subject to ignorance, weakness, and death.

This manifold expression of the Logos (on earth as well as in heaven, in Jesus as well as in the Father, in flesh as well as in the Spirit) occurred without damaging either the real divinity or the real humanity of Christ. So the Logos remained omnipotent, but the man Jesus was not so; the man Jesus lacked knowledge of many things, but the Logos possessed the full omniscience of God.

In other words, the incarnation did not add divine attributes to the human nature of Christ, but neither did it inhibit the freedom and power of his divine nature.

Chapter Fifteen

THE FORM OF A SERVANT

> ... taking the **_form of a servant_**, being born in the likeness of men, and being found **_fashioned like a man_**, he humbled himself and became obedient unto death (vs 7-8).

Paul uses two different and contrasting words – *morphe*, and *schema*. I have already explained that *morphe* means the essential nature of something, that which cannot be changed without destroying it. *Schema*, however, describes the outward "fashion" or "appearance" of something, that which *can* be changed without disturbing its real character.

Thus in winter, a clump of almond trees looks ugly, gnarled, sticky with globs of sap. But in spring it is transformed into a fairyland of pink and white blossoms, stunningly beautiful. The *morphe* of the trees remains unchanged, but the *schema* changes season by season. Likewise, the *morphe* of a woman remains the same throughout her life, but each stage of growth from infancy to old age, brings many changes in her "*schema*.

Those two words were often used carelessly, and in Greek texts their meanings are often blurred; but they never lost the basic distinction between *inner substance* and *outer shape*, between unalterable form and variable figure. And there seems no doubt that Paul intended that distinction to be recognised when he said that Christ took the *morphe* of a servant, but only the *schema* of a man.

THE "FORM OF A SERVANT"

Christ did not exchange the form of God for the form of a servant, as some have thoughtlessly claimed. Rather, being still in the form of God, he was yet willing to humble himself and to assume the form of a servant (Lu 22:27; and many other references).

That was the real *kenosis*.

From the place of highest authority, where the entire universe was absolutely subject to his will, he voluntarily embraced a state of subjection, in which he himself was obliged to render obedience to many – his parents (Lu 2:51); the government (Mt 17:24-27); the Father (He 10:7,9).

This was not merely adopting the "behaviour pattern" of a servant, as a kind of temporary expedient; rather, Christ embraced the very "form" or *morphe* of a servant. He assumed an actual servant nature, toward both God and man (Mt 22:21; 20:28).

But notice, a "servant" nature is not a "servile" nature. He was no slave. There was no compulsion laid upon his service. He was not a "servant" because he was driven to lowly employment by forces beyond his control. Rather he *chose* to serve. It was a voluntary expression of what has always been the true character of divine love.

In fact, Christ took on the form of a servant at the time of his *kenosis* only in relation to his appearance among men. In relation to the Godhead, the *morphe* of a servant has eternally been an integral part of the Divine nature. The one new thing created by the *kenosis* was that God, who from the beginning of history had been revealing himself to man in this servant role (but without adequate response), was now incarnate among men unmistakably as a servant.

Thus all excuse has been removed from proud man. The "form" of God and the "form" of a servant are now shown to be one. Those who would become partakers of the divine nature (2 Pe 1:4) may do so only via this example set by Christ of humility (1 Pe 2:21; Ph 2:1-7). All who thought that the proper image of God was one of power, privilege, and pomp, have had their abysmal error exposed. The chief characteristic of godliness is not sovereignty, but loving service.

THE "FASHION OF A MAN"

The changeable part of the *kenosis* was the appearance of Christ in *"the likeness (schema/fashion) of a man"* (Ph 2:7). Through the incarnation the Logos was united with human nature, and, in all of his expression of himself through the man Jesus, was content to function within the ordinary limitations of that nature.

How severe these limitations are is difficult for us to appreciate. William Hendriksen writes –

> (Christ) assumed human nature, not in the condition in which Adam had it before the Fall, nor in the condition in which Christ himself now has it in heaven, nor in the condition in which he will reveal it on the day of his glorious return, but in its fallen and therefore weakened condition, burdened with the results of sin (Is 53:2). [83]

Paul also reminds us that *"God sent his own Son in the likeness of sinful flesh"* (Ro 8:3). This does not mean, of course, that there was any sin in Christ, but only, as far as his human appearance and powers were concerned, that he reduced himself to our fallen condition. His state become one of "servitude and subjection, unattractiveness and lack of distinction," which are all characteristics of the debilitated human nature Christ adopted (J.J. Muller). As someone has said –

> He who had formerly existed in a manner equal to that of the exalted God, now humbled

---

[83]   Op.cit., pg. 100.

himself to exist in a manner equal to that of a fallen man.

But Paul is careful to say that Christ was born in the "fashion," not the "form," of a fallen man. Jesus was willing to live within the limitations that had been imposed on his fallen forefather, Adam, but he could not accept Adam's inner sinful nature. He took the "form" of a servant, for this is an eternal expression of God's nature; but only the "fashion" of a fallen man, for this had to change in the resurrection (Ac 2:23-24).

Now if Jesus lived within our human limitations, then he could not have made use of any powers that are not available to other men. Whatever spiritual or supernatural powers he used must have been of a kind that other people could have received and used as well as he. That this was actually the case is shown by Jesus' own words to his disciples –

> *Truly, truly, I say to you, he who believes in me will also do the works that I do; and greater works than these will he do, because I go to the Father (Jn 14:12).*

This matter of the limitations imposed on Christ during the incarnation is a difficult one. How could he at the same time have been the limitless Logos and the limited Jesus?

It is plain from the gospels that Jesus of Nazareth did not express, at least in any continual sense, any of those attributes that are typically divine – omnipotence, omnipresence, omniscience, and the like. But the question is – *did he at any point in his life ever possess them; and if he did possess them, did he ever use them; or if he did not possess them, how did he do his mighty works?*

The best answer to such questions would seem to be –

- Christ was conscious of his celestial identity as the Logos, and knew that as the Logos he could exercise unlimited personal power – but only at the cost of destroying his human identity.

That is why the Devil tempted him to resume his deity and to use *divine* powers to save his life – *"If you are the Son of God, command this stone to become bread."* But Jesus saw through the trap, and insisted that he was on earth as a man, not as God. He replied, *"<u>Man</u> shall not live by bread alone."*

He refused to be enticed into using anything beyond human resources to resist Satan's attacks.

Yet Satan apparently believed that had Jesus chosen to utilise them, heavenly powers *were* available to him, and that Jesus *knew* these powers were at his disposal.

There are some passages which do seem to imply the exercise of some divine attributes; but closer examination reveals a better explanation of his powers –

- <u>Luke 6:19</u>. The "power" referred to here is more likely to have been the power of the Holy Spirit than some kind of personal inner energy (see the following paragraph). The same comment applies to *John 1:48-49; 2:11; 4:17-18; 11:41-44; Matthew 17:27*.

- <u>John 2:24-25</u>. This probably means no more than that Jesus knew human nature; he had a shrewd perception of what man was like.

- <u>John 3:13</u> (AV). The words *"who is in heaven"* are not in all MSS, and appear to be an embellishment added by some scribe; in any case, they probably refer to Christ's position at the time John wrote his gospel, rather than at the time of Jesus' discussion with Nicodemus.

- <u>John 14:9</u>. I have already discussed the sense in which the incarnate Christ may be said to have revealed the Father, and it does not require that Jesus should have exercised some unique attribute of deity.

- <u>*Matthew 21:2; 26:17-19*</u>. It is not necessary to suppose that these events required supernatural knowledge – other explanations are possible. Even if a miracle of prescience is involved, it could be more readily explained as revelation given by the Holy Spirit than as a demonstration of personal omniscience by Jesus. The same applies to those occasions when he spoke as a prophet (e.g. Mt 24:3 ff).

- <u>Other references</u> – such as *Matthew 11:27; Mark 1:1; John 1:14; 5:19-24; 13:1-3; Romans 1:4; Colossians 1:15-16* – do not describe Christ as he was during the incarnation, but refer either to his pre-existent state, his present state, or to his eternal identity as the Logos.

So none of those references prove that Jesus of Nazareth ever used divine powers, that is, powers that are not available to other godly people, to fulfil all that the Father had ordained for him in his life and ministry. If the calling or purpose of God in your life or mine should require the use of such powers, then, through Holy Spirit baptism, they are available to us (Ac 1:8). The one exception in the life of Christ was in fact after his death, when he proved that he was truly the Son of God by calling his life back again (Ro 1:4; Jn 10:18).

A MAN FULL OF THE SPIRIT

Scripture, then, shows that Jesus depended upon the Holy Spirit for power to complete his mission – *Isaiah 11:1-2; 42:1-7; 61:1 ff; Matthew 12:28; Luke 4:16-21; Acts 10:38*; etc. His miracles were also a response to faith and prayer, in dependence upon God (Mk 9:29; Jn 11:41,42), hence they could be hindered by unbelief (Mk 6:5-6; Mt 13:58). See also *John 3:34; 5:19-20; 8:28; 15:15; 17:1,8*; and *Acts 2:22*.

It is particularly significant that Jesus wrought no miracle until after he was filled with the Holy Spirit (Lu 4:14, 40-41).

Thus, in all that he did for our redemption, Jesus acted as a man empowered by the Holy Spirit; that is, he used the same means available to you and me – and using them, he triumphed – thus perfectly representing us in the work that he did (cp. again Jn 14:12).

Whatever mysteries are created by the surrender by Jesus of the attributes of his deity, nothing can alter the gospel witness that he was a *man* filled with Holy Spirit, and that the power of the Spirit was the source of his miracles. This is the plain explanation of all his works; it is the one Jesus himself gave for at least some of his miracles; and it seems better to apply this to all his miracles than to explain some in terms of the Spirit, and others in terms of his own innate power. In general, if a natural and simple explanation is adequate, then it is unwise to look for a more complex, or higher, one. (84)

Jesus never claimed omniscience. He claimed to know the Father as no other knew him (Mt 11:27); but he also admitted that his knowledge as incarnate Son was limited in so important a matter as the time of his return (Mt 24:36; Mk

---

(84) One of the common rules of theology and philosophy is known as *Ockham's Razor* (from William of Ockham, c. 1290-1349). It gains that quaint name from the notion that all unnecessary complications must be "shaved" or removed from an argument. In other words, truth is found in the simplest explanation adequate to explain a given set of data. The Razor is often expressed by the aphorism: "Entities must not be multiplied beyond necessity;" or perhaps more simply, "What can be done with few is done in vain with more." It is sometimes called also *The Principle of Parsimony*.

13:32). This limited knowledge of Jesus is also suggested in the following – [85]

- he was sometimes surprised and disappointed (Mt 8:10; 26:40; Mk 11:13; Lu 2:49).
- he gained information in the usual manner, by hearing and seeing (Mt 4:12; 14:13; Mk 2:17; 5:30; Jn 1:38).
- he asked questions because he needed an answer (Mt 9:28; 16:13,15; Mk 6:38; 8:23; 9:21; Lu 8:30; Jn 11:34).
- he developed mentally, and learned by experience, just as we do (Lu 2:52; He 5:8).
- he sought guidance from God in prayer (Lu 5:16; 6:12).
- the necessity of Calvary was not fully clear to him (Mt 26:39); and when he became convinced of it, he was not sure that he could endure it (vs 42,44; and cp. He 5:7).

For all those reasons, scripture is well able to say that Christ has set us an example that we too, in the power of the Holy Spirit, can emulate! (1 Pe 2:21) Thus both the character of Jesus and his deeds are wrought in us and through us by the Holy Spirit (Ga 5:22-23; 1 Co 12:7-11).

SOLUTIONS TO DIFFICULTIES

Having got this far in our study of the *kenosis* of Christ it is now time to consider some problems and their answers ....

---

(85) Based on a paragraph by Alfred Garvie, in an article on the *kenosis*, in Hastings, op.cit., Vol 1; pg. 928.

THE TRANSFIGURATION OF CHRIST

– Matthew 17:1-9; Mark 9:2-10; Luke 9:28-36.

Some have suggested that the *transfiguration* was an occasion when Jesus did for a time resume his former glory. For a brief period, there on the mountain, he ceased to be an ordinary man and stood (they say) as God upon the earth. But note –

- Although, in the light of other things Jesus said and did (especially his resurrection), the transfiguration was rightly seen by the disciples as a *confirmation* of his divine identity, the record of the event itself makes no mention of this.

Furthermore, there are other similar instances in scripture where there is no possible suggestion that the subjects were divine (Ex 34:29; Da 12:3; Ac 26:13-14).

- Albert Barnes writes –

  The word 'transfigure' means 'to change the appearance or form.' It does not denote a change of the 'substance' of a thing, but simply of its appearance. It puts on a new aspect. What this change was, we are expressly told – *(1)* his face shone as the sun; that is, with a peculiar brightness ... *(2)* The second change was that of his garments. They were white as the light ... There is no evidence here that what is commonly said of him is true, that his body was so changed as to show what his glorified body is. His body, so far as the sacred writers inform us, underwent no change. All this splendour and glory was a change in appearance only. The scriptures should be taken just as they are, without any attempt to affix a meaning to them which the sacred writers did not intend. [86]

- No doubt it is expedient, now that Christ is again dwelling in equality with the Father, to see in the transfiguration at least a *symbol* of his eternal and personal magnificence; but that does not seem to have been the original intention of that display of glory.

The transfiguration is seldom alluded to in the NT, and in fact the only explicit reference (apart from the gospels) is in *2 Peter 1:16-18*, where Peter states that it was not an act of self-revelation on the part of Christ, but rather an act of the Father – *"(Christ) received honour and glory from God the Father."*

The specific context of the transfiguration is that of the Messianic kingdom, not that of the deity of Christ. This is shown by the following –

- The transfiguration was a direct consequence of Jesus' own words, *"There are some standing here who will not taste death before they see the Son of man coming in his kingdom"* (Mt 16:28). Peter (who was one of those "standing there," and who was with Christ on the mountain) clearly believed that in the transfiguration he had seen the Messianic king coming in his glory – *"We made known to you the power and coming of our Lord Jesus Christ, (for) we were eyewitnesses of his majesty"* (2 Pe 1:16).

- The words spoken by the Father (*"This is my beloved Son, with whom I am well pleased"* – Mt 17:5) were a

---

(86) Notes on the New Testament; Kregel Publications, Grand Rapids, Michigan; 1966 reprint; in loc.

clear affirmation (as I showed you earlier) that Christ was the Messiah.

- When the NT writers wanted proof of the deity of Christ, they referred, not to his transfiguration, but to his resurrection (Ro 1:4; and many others).

So, although the transfiguration does provide a beautiful illustration, even a sign, of the deity of Christ, it seems better to suppose that its real purpose was – *(1)* to confirm to the disciples the Messianic identity of Christ; *(2)* to mark a crisis a point in his ministry – for from this time (having discussed his coming "departure" with Moses and Elijah – Lu 9:31) he set his face steadfastly toward Calvary and the final act in his Messianic mission.

The transfiguration, therefore, did not involve the sudden calling up by Christ of latent divine powers, nor did it in any way disturb his humanity. It was not in itself proof of the deity of Christ, nor a sign of that deity.

THE SINLESSNESS OF CHRIST

If Jesus was truly a man, and if he never once during the incarnation used any personal divine power, how was he able to maintain a state of sinlessness? Is absolute impeccability possible for any human being, even for Jesus of Nazareth? Surely here we have a point in the life of Jesus at which he had no choice but to draw upon the inherent resources of his deity? James Stalker provides a fine answer –

> Some have indeed held (that the sinlessness of Christ) directly proves his divinity; because, they have argued, the moral force of mere manhood would not have been equal to the task of maintaining a life of sinlessness in a sinful world. If even Adam, in an empty and sinless world, fell, then what chance was there of another, standing in a world so corrupt and a society so perverted as that in which Jesus lived, moved, and had his being?

To bring the divine nature, however, into play to account for the sinlessness, would obscure the reality of the temptation of Jesus; and it obscures the vital truth that his sinlessness was not only a gift but an attainment, which he had to secure afresh on every step of a human development, and which rendered him supremely well-pleasing to his Father in heaven. God gave the Spirit without measure to him (Jn 3:34); and, by constantly receiving this divine communication and giving it free play within him, he garrisoned his human nature against the advances of sin. This is enough to account for his constant victory over temptation. [87]

And Barry Chant [88] raises and answers another question – *How did Christ remain sinless before he was baptised in the Holy Spirit?* <u>Answer</u> – Before receiving the Spirit, Christ was in the same position as a born-again believer. From the day of his birth he was born of the Spirit (Lu 1:34-35). Thus, he was able, through his relationship to God as the Son of God, to maintain his sinlessness. See *Romans 8:12-17*, where sonship is identified with putting to death the deeds of the flesh.

THE TEMPTATIONS OF CHRIST

If Jesus really was God incarnate, how valid were the temptations that confronted him each day, and was it ever possible for him to sin? After all, the Bible does say, *"God cannot be tempted with evil"* (Ja 1:13).

---

(87)   Hastings; op.cit., Vol 2; pg. 639.
(88)   *Op. cit.*, pg. 31.

WAS HE REALLY TEMPTED?

The issue here is – since God, by the very nature of his being, cannot possibly sin, nor have the slightest inclination to sin, how could Jesus (the God-man) have been subject to real temptation? Surely temptation is meaningful only where sin is possible. If there is no possibility of yielding, then temptation is a futile game, a pretence, a fiction.

Every effort to solve this problem has so far been unsatisfactory. Every solution tends to fall into one heresy or another – perhaps Christ was not altogether *"without sin;"* or, perhaps the temptations were actually unreal; or, perhaps Jesus was not truly divine; or not truly human?

Yet scripture is plain enough. It insists that Jesus was indeed bitterly and fiercely tempted, *"just as we are"* (He 2:18; 4:13; Lu 22:28; Mt 4:1-11; plus many other references, which describe opposition, pressure, frustration, disappointment, grief, and the like, that frequently beset Jesus.) It is impossible to deny the genuine force of these temptations without stripping all meaning from the various accounts.

It is true that *"God cannot be tempted"*. Why? Because *omniscience* perfectly understands the real nature of every object, the source and destiny of all things, and the past, present, and future ramifications of every action, word, and thought. It is therefore impossible for an omniscient mind to make a wrong decision, or to will to do falsely, or to be enticed to evil by a mind less than itself.

Likewise *omnipotence* cannot be placed under any kind of pressure or test, it cannot show itself weak, it can never be defenceless, nor surrender any of its limitless power. There is simply no temptation able to touch the Almighty!

Temptation becomes possible only where –
- There is limited knowledge – as Jesus showed in the Garden of Gethsemane (Mt 26:37-46; Lu 22:40-44).

- There is limited power – as Jesus experienced when he was weak with hunger after his long fast (Mt 4:2-3).
- Moral development is incomplete, so that moral character needs to be tested and confirmed.

Just as Jesus' body and mind followed the normal processes of human growth, so also did his moral and spiritual development (Lu 2:52; 4:1-2,14; He 5:8); and during that time of character growth he remained susceptible to temptation.

Temptation was directed at Christ in the same two ways it comes to us – appealing to desire, and to fear. So, at the beginning of his ministry, Satan in the wilderness enticed the *desires* of Jesus – for bread, for acclaim, for glory. And at the end of his ministry, Satan in the garden stirred the *fears* of Christ – of being touched by sin, of the unknown, of death. In both of those major temptations Jesus triumphed through the power of the Holy Spirit, and the angels ministered to him (Mk 1:13; Lu 22:43).

> Many people, confusing temptation with sin, are troubled at the thought that Jesus could be tempted. It must be recognised that temptations are appeals to legitimate needs and desires. The error is in suggesting that these desires should be fulfilled in a way contrary to God's will. It is when men place the fulfilment of their own wills before the will of God and give way to the temptation that there is sin (Ja 1:14,15). Jesus steadfastly refused to satisfy his needs or fulfil his purpose in any way

that would for one moment take him outside the will of the Father. (89)

So the answer to the first question must be a firm – "Yes, Jesus was really tempted; yet he overcame every attack, and remained quite without sin!"

But this still leaves the problem –

WAS IT POSSIBLE FOR JESUS TO SIN?

Louis Berkhof claims –

> Christ could avoid sinning, and did actually avoid it, but also it was *impossible* for him to sin because of the essential bond between the human and the divine natures.

That view leaves an unanswerable question, which Berkhof himself raises –

> But ... the problem remains – how was it possible that one who ... was actually constituted (so that he) could not sin nor even have an inclination to sin, nevertheless be subject to real temptation? (90)

Berkhof (along with many other theologians) offers no reply to his question. He thinks the dilemma has no solution. To him it is inconceivable that Jesus could have done anything else but withstand temptation. Yet how can temptation be real to a man who cannot possibly yield to it?

---

(89) P.C. Johnson, <u>Zondervan Pictorial Encyclopedia of the Bible</u>; Vol 5; Zondervan Publishing House, Grand Rapids, Michigan; 1975; pg. 802.

(90) <u>Systematic Theology</u>; Banner of Truth Trust, London; 1976; pgs. 318,338.

I think it should be noted, however, that Berkhof's problem does not rise out of scripture so much as it is a product of dogmatic theology. (91) The biblical witness, taken at face value simply declares that the pre-existent Christ, through the *kenosis*, did take on the "fashion" of a man, and was thus subject to the full gamut of earthly temptations. (92) Presumably, then, sin was a possibility for Jesus of Nazareth. But how that could occur, or what the effect of it might have been, or, for that matter, whether or not it truly was possible, is nowhere addressed in scripture.

The same kind of response could be made to the following passage from Lewis Chafer –

> A serious question, quite hypothetical, yet vital, arises whether Christ, being human, had the ability to sin. Was he peccable or impeccable? ... There are those who, desiring to accentuate the reality of Christ's humanity, have taught that he could have sinned ... apparently without due regard for all that is involved ... (It) is essential to recognise that ... an unfallen human being may sin; and from this it may be reasoned, were there no other factors to be considered, that the unfallen humanity of Christ could have sinned. It is not at this point that error intrudes. If isolated and standing alone, it is claimed that the humanity of Christ, being unsupported, could have willed against

---

(91) See again the *Preface* to Emmanuel – Part One.

(92) Excepting of course, those temptations we suffer that arise from a nature that is already fallen and sinful. From those temptations Jesus was plainly exempt. This may be the better meaning of He 4:15, *"tempted as we are* (except that he was) *apart from sin."* Remember also that temptation could be addressed to his human nature, but never to his divine nature.

God as Adam did. The misleading fallacy is that the humanity of Christ could ever stand alone and unsupported by his deity.

With Adam there was but one nature and it could stand in no other way than unsupported and alone. The humanity of Christ was not and could not be, divorced from deity ... Because of the unity of his Person, his humanity could not sin without necessitating God to sin. From such a conclusion all devout persons must shrink with holy fear ... This vexing problem is thus reduced to the simple question whether God could sin; for Jesus Christ is God. If it be admitted that God cannot – not merely would not – sin, it must be conceded that Christ could not – not merely would not – sin ...

Since God cannot be compromised with evil, the normal capacity of unfallen humanity to sin, as that humanity was represented in Christ, could never be exercised to the slightest degree. An unfallen nature, which is welded to God cannot sin since God cannot sin ... Those who assert that Christ could have sinned must aver either that Christ is not God or that God may himself be ruined by sin ... If Christ could have sinned on earth, he can sin in heaven. He is the same yesterday, today, and forever. If he can sin now, there is no final assurance that he will not sin and thus bring every human hope based on redemption into ruin. Such conclusions are an insult against God and cannot be tolerated by those who bow in

> adoration before the Christ of God ... there is no logic which is more inexorable than this. (93)

The true issue, as I have already suggested, seems to be whether to be controlled by the "inexorable logic" of dogmatic theology, or by the clear record of the gospels. It is certainly difficult not to be deeply moved by the kind of arguments raised by Dr Chafer. Every godly soul must be inclined to accept them, for the very idea of Jesus sinning is indeed repulsive. But I find myself stumbling over the equally forceful proposition that temptation is a farce if yielding is impossible. And it can hardly be doubted that scripture tells us how bitterly Jesus suffered when he was tempted. (Lu 22:41-44; He 2:18; 5:7-9;)

The ancients, in their endless debates on this mystery, summed the matter up in two neat phrases – either the Saviour was "not able to sin," or he was "able not to sin." The first emphasises the union of Christ with God; the second, his union with man. The debate was never finally resolved.

Since my own disposition is toward biblical rather than dogmatic theology, I am prone to believe that as part of his *kenosis*, and as inexplicable as this might be, Jesus really did make himself vulnerable to temptation.

Another suggestion has been made, that while Jesus was in fact *unable* to sin, yet because he had (through the incarnation) voluntarily abandoned his omniscience, he did not *know* that he was unable to sin! So the temptation was still real. But this ignores the fact that *Satan* knew the real origin of Jesus and would hardly have bothered to tempt him if there was no possibility of Christ yielding (cp. Mk 1:24; Lu 4:34; Mt 4:3).

---

(93) <u>Systematic Theology</u>; Dallas Seminary Press, Dallas, Texas; 8 vols; 1962; Vol 1, pg. 393-394; Vol V, pg. 5,50-51,78.

It seems difficult then to deny that while sin is plainly impossible for the eternal Logos, it must have been possible for the incarnate Christ. G.A. Turner writes –

> The writer to the Hebrews stated that (Jesus) was tempted in all points as we are (2:18; 4:15), implying that the temptation was real and that he could have yielded, just as anyone could yield to temptation. To deny that Jesus could have sinned is to deny his humanity and to fall into the error of Docetism, which maintains that his humanity was only an appearance and not actually real. Because Jesus was truly human he could have yielded to these temptations (in the wilderness) and others like them and forfeited his messiahship and sonship. He refrained from using his divine status to minimise the temptations, but permitted them to be felt in their full force. Thus he was truly man as he was truly God. (94)

HOW DID HE PARDON SIN?

When Christ forgave the sins of people around him, would not this have involved drawing on his divine attributes? Surely he could forgive sin only by speaking and acting as God? And if that is so, then does it not destroy the whole argument about Christ never using any divine attributes during the incarnation?

Solution – forgiving sin may be seen as a matter of divine *nature* rather than divine *attributes*. It was an act of grace, not of power. It was an expression of love, made in the knowledge of his eternal identity; it did not require an act of deity. This is perhaps a forced distinction, but it is the only

---

(94) Zondervan, op.cit., Vol 1, pg. 802. On *Docetism*, see *Chapter Three* above.

feasible way to define the basis on which Jesus of Nazareth was able to forgive sin.

WHY BOTH GOD AND MAN?

If Christ did not once use his divine attributes during the incarnation, why did he *need* to be God and man? Could not a holy man chosen by God have done the same redeeming work?

Those questions have already been answered above in various ways. But here is a closing paragraph on the matter –

> As a man, Jesus had the right to represent fallen man. But his single life would then have been sufficient to be the substitute for only one other man. For the lives of *all* men to be saved, an equal number of sinless men would have needed to substitute their lives for those of the sinners. But because he was also God, Christ had not only the *right* to save all men, but also the *ability* to do so. The life of God is worth more than the sum total of all other lives. Thus –
>
> *All this is from God, who through Christ reconciled us to himself, not counting their trespasses against them ... For our sake he made him to be sin who knew no sin, so that in him we might become the righteousness of God (2 Co 5:17-21).* [95]

---

(95) Barry Chant, op.cit., pg. 32.

Chapter Sixteen

THE MAN OF CALVARY

My previous chapters have in one way or another all been a discussion of the two great mysteries that are attached to Christ

- the mystery of the **_union_** of his two natures (the divine and the human)
- the mystery of his **_person_** (that is, his identity as the eternal Logos).

Christians have tended to emphasise one or the other of these two mysteries, and hence to develop different ideas about the manner in which Christ saves us.

This chapter will explore the contrast between those two viewpoints, and how they reveal excitingly different aspects of the great salvation God has wrought for us in Christ.

THE PURPOSE OF THE INCARNATION

Teachers who emphasise the mystery of Christ's **_identity_** tend to focus their attention on the personal saving acts of Christ – especially on the events surrounding his passion. They concentrate on *Calvary*, not Bethlehem. Salvation for them is primarily located in the death, resurrection, and ascension of the Divine Saviour. His incarnation is important mainly because it was a necessary prelude to the sacrificial drama that occurred at the end of his life.

Those who emphasise the mystery of Christ's two **_natures_** tend to focus their attention on the fact that *"the Word became flesh and dwelt among us"* (Jn 1:14). They concentrate on *Bethlehem*, not Calvary. Salvation for them is primarily located in the fusion of the divine with the human in Christ. People are saved when in turn they too are absorbed into the divine. The passion of Christ is important mainly because it was the ultimate demonstration of his union with his fallen people.

The first theory we may call *"salvation by atonement."* The second, *"salvation by incarnation."* There is no doubt that both concepts are scattered through the pages of scripture. Which of the two is reckoned to be the most prominent will probably depend on which pair of eyes is looking for the evidence!

In general, Christians who are guided by the teaching of the Reformers (Luther, Calvin, and their ilk), that is, "evangelical" Christians, are likely to emphasise the *atonement*; other Christians are likely to emphasise the *incarnation*.

To the ***first***, the cross was a once-for-all event, and salvation is now expressed by personal faith and devotion, and by a piety that tends to separate itself from *"the world"* and from all that belongs to it. To the **second**, the cross was a symbol of the perpetually suffering Christ, who still lives and dies among men through his church, and salvation means deeply integrating Christ with every part of our human experience.

The ***first*** views salvation as an essentially private matter, to be determined by each person alone in the presence of God. It is concerned more with individual souls than with mankind as a whole. The **second** views salvation as an essentially corporate matter to be discovered by each individual in association with the larger company of God's people. It is more concerned with the redemption of human society than with individual perfection.

The ***first*** finds its dynamic in the concept of Christ as our **Redeemer**, ransoming us from sin by substituting himself for us on the cross. The **second** finds its dynamic in the concept of Christ as our **Exemplar**, whose incarnation compels a deep change of attitude and life-style in all who become his disciples.

The ***first*** tends toward detachment from the world and its affairs; the ***second*** tends toward involvement in the world and its affairs.

So then, when the *humanity* of Christ is emphasised, a spirituality develops that concentrates on the Christian's place in the world and in society. Christ is seen as being imminent in human affairs, while little stress is placed on his transcendent glory. He becomes a world-oriented Christ, found more on earth than in heaven. He can be seen in every slum, in the face of every outcast person. He is in the factories and farms. He can be found wherever there is true work to be done; and where there is humility or suffering, his voice of compassion can be heard. He can be found in his church, incarnate among his people, still working, witnessing, hurting, laughing, living, and dying, through them.

Conversely, when the *deity* of Christ is emphasised, a spirituality develops that concentrates, not on Christian involvement with humanity, but on each believer's personal spiritual development. The focus is other-worldly, directed more toward the City of God in heaven than the cities of men on earth. Christ becomes *transcendent* rather than imminent, and he is worshipped with an up-turned face of rapture more than with an out-turned face of compassion.

Those definitions, of course, are over-simplified; but I think they give a fair idea of the general trend of each kind of piety – the one more subjective and personal; the other more objective and corporate. You would rarely find one group altogether rejecting the concepts of the other. On the contrary, they usually endorse the scriptural truths of each other's position – yet still adhere to their own identity and style, and maintain their own emphasis.

Broadly speaking, this book reflects an "atonement" theory of salvation rather than an "incarnation" theory. Obviously, that emphasis stems from my particular background, training, and preference. But I feel it is important to devote at least a few paragraphs to the alternate emphasis – (96)

INCARNATION AS THE DYNAMIC OF SALVATION

Many of our popular hymns, whether consciously or not, reflect an incarnational dynamic –

> When I survey the wondrous cross,
> On which the Prince of glory died,
> My richest gain I count but loss,
> And pour contempt on all my pride.
> Were the whole realm of nature mine,
> That were an offering far too small;
> Love so amazing, so divine,
> Demands my soul, my life, my all. (97)

Notice that the emphasis in Isaac Watts' poem is not so much on a sinner standing before the cross and seeing there a Substitutionary Victim who is making formal atonement for sin; but rather, on a proud human heart being broken by the example of Christ, and then driven to follow in the Master's steps.

---

(96) I will write on only one aspect of "incarnational theory", namely its concept of spirituality in contrast with the concept of spirituality created by "atonement theory." An extensive discussion would include consideration of the larger issues of church and society, such as the attitude the church should have to war, poverty, revolution, capitalism, communism, politics, economics, etc. Such matters are beyond the scope of this book. Perhaps more pertinently, they are also outside my competence.

(97) Isaac Watts.

This idea is beautifully expounded by Richard Holloway in his book *"A New Heaven,"* [98] which explores the ramifications of incarnational salvation. With pungent insight, Holloway challenges contemporary society to look again at the Christ made flesh among us. I have used his book as a guide and corrective for the following paragraphs; however, my thoughts are directly dependent on his only where page numbers are cited. I say this to protect him from blame, not myself. He writes –

> (Incarnational theory) sees the work of Christ as having its effect by changing people's attitudes as they think about and contemplate the great loving sacrifice of Christ. As we study how he lived, we cannot but be moved by his great love and seek to copy it in our own lives. But there is more, even, than this. Our very understanding of God is altered, because the life and death of Jesus show us what God is like. He's our servant and our victim. He rescues us, ransoms us from the bondage of our anxious selfishness, not by an act of power and overwhelming justice, but by an act of self-emptying love. He woos us, this God of ours ... The cross is the final example of God's love – it is the action which finally secures our release from our own fears and loneliness ... (It) opens up for us the very heart of God, and what we see there is the unconquerable love which guides the universe, not with overwhelming power, but with invincible weakness, and it moves us to heartbroken love (pg. 38,39).

---

[98] Mowbray & Co Ltd; Oxford, UK; 1978. Some of the concepts of this book are quite different to those I have presented to you in either this book or its companion, but if you have an opportunity to read it you will find its pages stimulating and enriching.

THE HEART OF THE CROSS

So incarnational theory maintains that Calvary should be seen as just a vivid demonstration, at one point in history, of what men and women are doing to Christ every day. The cross shows us, inescapably, that we are compulsive murderers of our God. We attack him when we oppress our neighbour, when we ignore a widow's petition, when we turn our backs on those who are hungry and naked, when we ravage the natural creation, when we are brutal without reason to the creatures who inhabit the earth with us (Mt 25:45; Pr 12:10). We crucify Christ afresh when we ignore the gentle persuasion of the Holy Spirit, when we are indifferent in prayer, when we walk proudly and selfishly, when we violate the righteous command of God or further mar the image of God within us.

But Calvary is also a demonstration of how God responds to this perpetual betrayal – always with unending and unfaltering love. The power of the cross is the power of love. For it is this very love-example which impels us to loathe our greed, to discard our rebellion, to clothe our hearts with the same humble garment of self-sacrifice, and to go out and serve our neighbour.

CHANGED BY THE CROSS

"The universe," says Holloway, "is alive with the unending noise of hammer-blows" – the awful sound of Christ being crucified in every age, in every place. Man hates. But God loves. And we cannot weary his love. Rather, "it wears us down with its mute and eloquent acceptance of all the self-hatred we pour upon him" (pg. 46).

Love continually confronts us in Christ, persuading us to throw down our defences, to become like Jesus, *"who emptied himself, took the form of a servant, and was born in the likeness of man"* (Ph 2:5-7).

You should notice how Paul, in that profound description of the incarnation, associates salvation, not just with the death of the Saviour, but also with his birth and life. The idea is often conveyed that Jesus was just a *Teacher* during the three years of his public ministry, and that he became a *Saviour* only in the last three days of his life. It is thought that the cross alone, at the end of Christ's life, has grace to save fallen man. We should affirm rather that saving grace comes out of his entire life of humility, obedience, selfless service, and suffering. From at least the day of his baptism, all that Jesus did was salvific in its effect.

Paul then insists that this example of Christ should drive us to *"work out our own salvation with fear and trembling, for God is at work in us, both to will and to work for his good pleasure"* (vs 12-13).

How can this salvation be recognised? How can we gain it? What is God's good pleasure? The answer is clear. Salvation is not a single, complete event, but an ongoing thing. We have to work it in, and work it out, by striving to be like Jesus. This means, says Paul,

> *having the same love, being in full accord, doing nothing from selfishness or conceit, but in humility counting others better than ourselves, not looking to our own interest, but also to the interests of others (vs 2-4).*

The dynamic for all this comes out of our contemplation of the manner in which Christ shared our human condition in his birth, life, and ultimately, and most human of all, in his death.

THE CROSS AND THE INCARNATION

So the *cross* was not just a *postlude* to the incarnation; as though it were regrettable, but not really essential. Nor was the *incarnation* just a *prelude* to the cross; as though it were necessary, yet not an integral part of the passion. The cross and the incarnation are inseparable, for neither has any meaning without the other. Indeed the cross is the supreme proof of the incarnation, for it shatters any docetic ideas by its absolute demonstration of the real manhood of Christ. By being born, and by dying, Jesus utterly united himself with the humanity of each one of us. My salvation depends upon his real birth, and upon his real death.

We say that the cross has for all time changed things between God and man. But "we do not mean that it changed God's attitude towards us, (as though) he was bought off by the blood of Christ. We mean that God changed *our* attitude to him by placarding his love for us in the cross of Christ" (pg. 47).

Our response to this divine love draws us into fellowship with the people of God. We become members of the corporate "body" of Christ on earth, the church. Through the church we become participants in the incarnation of Christ. He becomes part of us. We become part of him. Our lives become a perpetual re-enactment of the life, the love, the passion, the resurrection, of Christ.

With Paul we are then able to cry –

> *I rejoice in my sufferings for your sake, and in my flesh I complete what is lacking in Christ's afflictions for the sake of his body, that is, the church (Cl 1:24).*

When Paul suffers, Christ suffers. When Paul is beaten by his enemies, Christ is beaten. What Paul achieves, Christ achieves. Christ is in Paul who is in Christ. We should make the same confession about ourselves.

This identification between the believer and Christ is possible because the church is his "body" – that is, the continuation on earth of the incarnation. The church is an inseparable part of Christ. It is the present locale of *"Emmanuel"* – *"God Among Us"*. Christ is among the sacraments, among the preaching of the Word, among our prayers and worship, among our service each to the other, among those who minister the grace of God. These things all become channels of salvation, because salvation is where Christ is; where Christ is not, there is no salvation.

So we become truly "the children of God" when we merge with the incarnation of the Child through hearty involvement with both the inner worship and outer witness of the church. If we share his incarnation on earth there will be no doubt about our sharing his glorification in heaven! (99)

INCARNATION AND THE EUCHARIST

This identification with Christ is well-expressed in the eucharist, where those who share in the cup and the broken bread, the emblems of Christ incarnate, must themselves be willing to be broken and distributed as bread to the world.

---

(99) Remember that in these paragraphs I am endeavouring to explain the "incarnational" theory of the life and death of Christ. I am sympathetic with this view without agreeing with its tendency to downplay the atoning power of the Cross. Concerning the atonement, Michael Christensen writes –

"Many theories have been advanced by Christians as to what the atonement means (eg. penal substitution, limited atonement, vicarious atonement, ransom to the Devil, satisfaction theory, moral influence theory), but theories are not to be confused with the reality itself. As Lewis says, 'A man can accept what Christ has done without knowing how it works.' Any explanation of the Atonement is at best only a reasonable approximation. Doctrinal statements never quite square with the absolute reality" (op.cit., pg. 33).

For a rather unique variant on "incarnational" atonement, see also C.S. Lewis, Mere Christianity, Book II, ch 4, *The Perfect Penitent*. According to Lewis, Christ's death is a perfect demonstration of the meaning of repentance, and of how we can crucify our own fallen natures, and discover a new life of godliness.

In the words of Augustine, "the work of the incarnation must go forward" through the church. And Holloway – "If we would really be found by God, therefore, we must let ourselves be taken; we must allow ourselves to be consecrated; we must prepare ourselves to be broken; and we must suffer ourselves to be given away. That is the Christian Way, and Christ warned us that it was narrow and little-travelled upon, yet it is the royal road to God" (pg. 79).

Without that kind of two-fold participation (personal and corporate) in the incarnation of Christ, we delude ourselves if we think that we are truly recipients of his full salvation. And this is an ongoing process. It may well begin with a deep crisis of personal commitment, one blazing moment in which we suddenly capture the vision of God and yield everything to him. But "conversion is not a single event … (it is) a dynamic activity in which the soul is slowly unselfed and remade, formed after the pattern of Jesus … The 'moment' we allow ourselves to be taken by God is (only) the entry into a process" (pg. 82).

This arduous and self-denying process was described by Jesus himself, when he answered a question about whether or not few would be saved –

> *Enter by the narrow gate, for the gate is wide and the way is easy that leads to destruction, and those who enter by it are many. For the gate is narrow and the way is hard, that leads to life, and those who find it are few … Strive* [100] *to enter by the narrow door; for*

---

(100) The Greek word is *agonidzomai*, from which comes our word "agonise." The Greek has the sense of "strain every nerve to enter," "struggle with all your being," "exert every possible effort." The same root word is used in Lu 22:44, *"being in an <u>agony</u> he prayed more earnestly."*

many, I tell you, will seek to enter and will not be able (Mt 7:13-14; Lu 13:24).

Does that seem terribly hard?

You are right, it is!

But wait a moment! Look again at Jesus. He faced a blackness far beyond anything we shall ever encounter, and he overcame it by trustful dependence on the love of his Father, and in the strength of the indwelling Holy Spirit. He was our true example. For he gained this magnificent victory, "not because he was God dressed up as a man, but because he was a man completely surrendered to God" (pg. 106).

He did not have access to some supernatural skill not available to us. He was not a superman. He used the same resources God is willing to give you and me. "It was the humanity of Christ that worked wonders, a humanity empowered by God, because it had been surrendered to God. And we are offered the same arrangement!" (pg. 106).

The challenge of the incarnation is that we should allow God to express his will and his wonderful works as perfectly through our bodies as he was able to do through the body of Jesus.

If I do not allow the living Christ to invade my flesh, and to incarnate himself again in me, then I am nothing, and all my claim of faith is become a sham.

> Man exists to be mastered by God –
> Thou mastering me
> God! giver of breath and bread;
> World's strand, sway of the sea;
> Lord of living and dead;
> Thou hast bound bones and veins in me,
> Fastened me flesh,
> And after it almost unmade, what with dread,

Thy doing – and dost thou touch me afresh?
Over again I feel thy finger and find thee. (101)

---

(101) Gerard Manley Hopkins, Poem #28, st 1

Chapter Seventeen

THE GOSPEL and THE WORLD

The entrance of Christ into the world must be seen as a confirmation of the OT dictum that the world as God made it is "good" – the earth and all its fulness are still the Lord's, the world and all who dwell therein (Ps 24:1).

So we reject the idea that the earth is evil, that God is wholly absent from the world, and that only those can find him who seek him mystically in heaven. But we also reject the opposite idea that God is so closely enmeshed with the creation, so intimately involved with human affairs, that only those can find him who seek him materially on earth –

- Because God is transcendent, in heaven, we are obliged to develop an "other-worldly" spirituality, based on a supernatural encounter with him through the new birth, baptism in the Spirit, prayer, personal devotion, rapturous worship.

- But also, because God is immanent, on earth, we must develop a spirituality that is "this-worldly," based on a natural encounter with him in society.

Thus we are called to war against the wretched effects of sin, struggling to alleviate poverty and to remove injustice, striving for ethnic reconciliation, caring about the ecology, the unemployed, the sick, and about everything in our human condition that bears the marks of sin. Thus we live out the incarnation – _individually_, pressing boldly into the holiest by faith; and _corporately_, by taking the example of the cross into the world around us.

The Bible clearly contains both of those aspects of spirituality – that which denies the world and separates from it; that which affirms the world and becomes involved in its reform.

There is an undeniable tension between the two concepts, and groups of Christians have often tended to espouse one of them to the near exclusion of the other. But true spirituality will surely find a way to combine them into a single expression of worship and witness.

It is not difficult to see that the NT (and especially the letters of Paul) emphasises a spirituality marked by such things as separation from the world, mystical union with Christ, charismatic worship of God. Its sharpest focus is on the cross, and on entrance into the new creation by the new birth. Yet Paul's letters still contain much instruction on how Christian life should be expressed in the world around us, especially in matters of our care of each other and compassion for our neighbours.

The spirituality of the NT cannot be cut off from the spirituality of the OT, which is strongly incarnational in its emphasis. The spirituality of the OT plainly underlies the NT, and is taken for granted by it, and is revealed by those places (several of which I have already mentioned) where the NT itself does reflect an incarnational spirituality.

The incarnational spirituality of the OT is based on the opening chapters of the Bible, which teach that God created the heavens and the earth, and that he is deeply concerned about, and intimately involved in, everything that happens in the world he has made (cp. the words of Jesus, spoken within the OT dispensation, Mt 10:29-31).

Beginning with the original creation as an act of God, and arguing from God's continued participation in earthly affairs, the OT writers (especially the prophets) insisted that the servants of God cannot separate themselves from the human scene, but must become partners with God in influencing every aspect of community life. They had to display their belief in the immanence of God in their world by their concern for social justice, alleviating the misery of the poor, defending widows, the oppressed – and so on. [102]

Observe also, that just as social concern is expressed in the pages of the *NT*, so also ecstatic religious experience is readily discoverable in the *OT*. The full message of the Bible is surely this, even if we do begin our spiritual experience with an intense personal encounter with God, yet the reality of our inner faith and of our private experience will be demonstrated only when we do as the incarnate Christ did, *"humble ourselves and take on the form of a servant."*

THE EXAMPLE OF JESUS

Consider this arresting statement –

> *Jesus, knowing that the Father had given all things into his hands, and that he had come from God and was going to God, rose from supper and ...*

Following those stunning words – that here is a man who knew he had come *from* God, and was going *to* God, and that the Father had given *all* things into his hands – which of the following would you expect to read? –

---

(102) One of the great scandals of the evangelical world is that so many "born again" preachers (and their people) scour the OT prophets only to find predictions they can match up with current newspaper headlines. They utterly fail to grasp the real message of the prophets: a declaration of the wrath of God upon Israel for that nation's woeful failure to correct the oppression, injustice, and idolatry, that were rife in every city and hamlet. If you have not realised this before, I invite you now to put this book aside, read right through two or three of the prophetic books (not looking for apocalyptic predictions), and really listen to what the prophets were saying to their society, and to ours.

> "Jesus rose, and sternly rebuked the disciples, because they failed to perceive his real identity, and did not render him proper honour."

> "Jesus rose, and gave an awesome display of his power, shaking the very earth by the immensity of his strength."

> "Jesus rose, shouted with a mighty voice, and summoned twelve legions of fiery angels to surround him in glittering battle array."

No! None of those things! In what seems to be an almost schizophrenic change of direction, a stupefying disjunction, John writes that Jesus,

> *knowing he had come from God and was going to God, rose from supper, laid aside his garments, and girded himself with a towel. Then he poured water into a basin, and began to wash the disciples' feet ... (13:3-5).*

Then the Master said,

> *I have given you an example, that you also should do as I have done to you (vs 15).*

Do you claim to have seen a vision of the Almighty? Do you reckon yourself to be born of God? Do you sing that your destiny is among the redeemed of the Lord, that you will surely possess a magnificent inheritance in the kingdom of God? Do you testify that, like Jesus, you "know" your identity in God, crucified, raised, and enthroned with Christ?

Do I know those things about myself? How then will I respond to this knowledge, that I have (in a spiritual sense) come *from* God and am going *to* God? With vaunting pride, sanctimonious indifference, or preoccupied piety?

If you and I reckon that we "know" as Jesus "knew", then let us do as Jesus did. Communion with the Father, revelation of the glorious position the believer has in Christ, a dynamic spiritual experience, a sense of indwelling divine power, will cause a true Christian to *"wash the disciples' feet"*! We do not want the kind of piety that cannot see the sorrow of God in the tears of an orphan, nor hear the plea of God in the groans of the oppressed, nor feel the ravishment of God in the pains of the tormented. But neither do we want the kind of piety that is all social action, scorning religious devotion, deriding the usefulness of prayer, turning the world itself into God.

Let us avoid both extremes. Godly involvement in social reform should spring out of a deep religious experience, just as true personal piety should lead to a concern for the renewal of society (cp. Mt 5:13-16; etc). Without that kind of dynamic balance, social reformation will soon decay into political revolution, personal renewal will soon debase into religious bigotry. If you want God's opinion about such people read *Isaiah 65:1-7*, especially *vs 5*.

The Lord's Prayer finely expresses this balance in two sentences –

> *Our Father who art in heaven, hallowed be thy name. Thy kingdom come, thy will be done, on earth as it is in heaven (Mt 6:9-10).*

Here is a heart of faith, hallowing the name of God, enjoying sweet communion with the Father – yet praying for the kingdom of God to dawn *today*, not tomorrow. Such a prayer pre-supposes that the one who so petitions will then get off his knees, go out, and see what he can do himself to hasten the realisation, right here on earth, of the kingdom of God.

AN IMPORTANT BALANCE

If we become engrossed in the humiliation of Christ, and look no further, we have failed in our study. Two important facts must be realised –

- to understand the doctrine of the incarnation is not sufficient – we must know the *Person* who was incarnate, for Jesus is not a theory to be analysed – he is a person to be accepted.

- all that Christ has done is for a purpose.

Why did God become man in the person of Jesus Christ? Here is a summary of the basic values wrought by Christ when he became flesh and dwelt among us – (103)

- ***Identification*** – to save men and women, God had to become identified with them. He had to take our sin upon himself. He had to share our guilt (although in himself guiltless) (2 Co 5:21; 1 Pe 2:24).

- ***Reconciliation*** – Jesus reconciled us to God (2 Co 5:19). Only one who could represent both parties (sinners and God) was in the perfect position to achieve this reconciliation.

- ***Participation*** – by becoming a man, Jesus shared intimately in human suffering, sorrow, and death (He 2:18; 4:15-16). We now know that *he* knows, he understands, he cares, he shares.

- ***Expiation*** – only as a man could he make lawful expiation for the sins of the people. The price necessary was human death. This could be paid only by one who fully shared our human nature (He 2:17).

- ***Impartation*** – he participated in our weakness and loss so that we could participate in his strength; he shared our poverty so that we could share his wealth (2 Co 8:9).

- ***Redemption*** – since we were enslaved by sin, a price had to be paid so that we could be bought back, or "redeemed," from this state of slavery. Jesus

---

(103) From Barry Chant, op.cit., pgs. 32,33.

purchased our redemption by the price of his own life, for nothing less was sufficient (1 Pe 1:18-19).

- **Substitution** – we were guilty of sin; we stood condemned, so Jesus became a man and took our place, taking the death penalty upon himself (Ro 5:6-8).

A mere man, even if he were perfect from his birth to his death, would not be an adequate ransom for more than one life. An angel, even of the highest order, would hardly suffice for the ransom of one soul. We need here a substitute whose offering is literally infinite in value so that the giving of his one life might indeed provide a ransom for the many ... We need one whose person is so great that the relatively brief time of his torment might be readily seen as equivalent to the eternal punishment and death which sin rightly deserves. No one but God himself satisfies these conditions – the immensity of the work of salvation demands the deity of the Saviour. [104]

- **Salvation** – only people need to repent, believe and be saved. Only God is able fully to repent and believe. But God has no need to. He did so, however, on our behalf, by becoming human in Christ (Ro 5:6).

- **Justification** – only by fully keeping the law can anyone be lawfully justified. By becoming a man and fully keeping the law, Jesus achieved complete justification on our behalf (Ro 5:22 ff).

---

(104) Dr R. Nicole, in an essay, *Jesus Christ, The Unique Son of God*, in Let The Earth Hear His Voice; World Wide Publications, Minneapolis, Minnesota; 1975; pg. 1043.

CONCLUSION

All the reasons for the incarnation can be expressed in the pithy words of several of the creeds –

Christ was made flesh for us men and for our salvation.

The emphasis here is plain – it was vital that Jesus act strictly as representative man in fulfilling the requirements of our redemption. Had he even once stepped outside the boundaries of his humanity to use his own divine powers, then the entire work of salvation would have been invalidated. He might as well have never become man at all. But his human nature, trusting in the grace of God, infused by the Holy Spirit, was equal to every demand placed upon it.

True, in the days of his flesh, and under fearful attack by the spirits of wickedness, Jesus had to offer up many prayers and supplications, with loud cries and tears, to the Father who was able to save him from death. But, because of his godly fear, he was heard, and the Father delivered him (He 5:7). And now, having been made perfect, Jesus has become the source of eternal salvation to all who obey him (vs 8-9).

The next two chapters offer some practical applications of the doctrine of the absolute pre-eminence of Christ as Son of Man and Son of God.

Chapter Eighteen

THE FULNESS OF CHRIST

The supreme god of the Olympian pantheon was Zeus, who reigned in awful splendour from his throne on the mountain peak. But he had not always been so powerful. Indeed, when he was still an infant his life came into great peril. He was rescued (says the myth) by a shepherd maiden who hid him in a cave, safe from his enemies, and fed him on goat's milk.

Years later, when he was fully grown, and had seized control over the Olympian realm, having forced all the other deities to submit to his rule, and destroyed any who resisted him, Zeus resolved to reward the maiden whose compassion for a helpless baby had preserved him. Her name was Amalthea, which means *tenderness*.

Zeus broke one horn off Amalthea's goat, whose milk had nourished him, and gave it mystical power, so that from its mouth would pour whatever its owner wanted. That horn became known as the *Cornucopia*, from two Latin words that mean the *Horn of Plenty*. Today it is usually portrayed as an elegant curving horn with a profusion of fruit tumbling out of its open mouth. Whatever the maiden desired, she had but to shake the horn, and behold, her wish would materialise!

In the ancient Greek world another word was also associated with the *Cornucopia*. It is the word *pleroma*, which means *fulness, abundance, overflowing riches*, and it was used (among other things) to describe the profligate gifts produced by the Horn of Plenty. Paul uses *pleroma* twice in our text – [105]

> *The <u>fulness</u> of the Godhead dwells in Christ bodily, and that same <u>fulness</u> has been given to you through your union with him (Cl 2:9-10).*

With extraordinary daring, Paul applies the same word to us he does to Christ – *"fulness – pleroma"*. That is, as surely as Christ possesses all the **<u>fulness</u>** of the Godhead bodily, so we too bodily possess all the **<u>fulness</u>** of Christ

The statement is so bold that many translators prefer to use one word for Christ and a different one for us –

> *For in him dwelleth all the <u>fulness</u> of the Godhead bodily, And ye are <u>complete</u> in him, which is the head of all principality and power. (KJV)*

> *For in Him dwells all the <u>fulness</u> of the Godhead bodily; and you are <u>completed</u> in Him, who is the head of all principality and power. (EMTV)*

> *For the full content of divine nature lives in Christ, in his humanity, and you have been given full life in union with him. (GNB)*

> *For it is in Christ that the Godhead in all its <u>fulness</u> dwells embodied; it is in him you have been bought to <u>fulfilment</u>. (REB)*

In the Greek text of Colossians, however, the same word, *pleroma*, with its sense of *extravagant abundance*, is used of

---

(105) I am not, of course, suggesting even remotely that Paul reckoned there was any truth in the old, and foolish, myth. I use it only to illustrate the meaning of *pleroma*, and the use it had in the ancient world.

both Christ and us, and any good translation should clearly reflect that startling fact.

Perhaps Jesus had a similar picture in mind when he used the expression *"more abundantly"* (Jn 10:10). The sense is that there is nothing parsimonious in what God has done for us in Christ, but rather it is so bountiful that it defies all measurement!

Somewhere I have heard the word translated as, *"we have been filled full"* in Christ; the idea being that we are not merely filled, but filled over and over again, filled to overflowing, and even beyond! Take a bucket and fill it with tennis balls. It is full, but not yet *filled-full*. Pack in a pile of marbles. It is even more full, but not yet *filled-full*. Shake into the bucket as many ball-bearings as it will hold, then sand, then powder. It is even more full than it was before, but not yet *filled-full*, for it still has room for water, then salt, and several other solubles! Eventually it will irresistibly overflow. Then indeed it may be said to be *filled-full*! So we have a shadowy picture of what God has given us in Christ.

What is this remarkable fulness? The following pages deal with just two areas where the fulness of Christ is sufficient for the emptiness that was in our souls –

THE RIGHTEOUSNESS OF CHRIST – SUFFICIENT FOR YOUR SIN

Perhaps the most pressing question in life is this – where lies the source of righteousness? For without a sense of righteousness there can be no peace, nor any hope of heaven. So pressing is this inner urge for holiness that people in every generation and every culture have sometimes resorted to the most extreme measures to gain it. A tragic and terrible example of this behaviour occurs in scripture, in the several passages that refer to people burning their children alive as a sacrifice to the gods (Le 18:21; De 12:31; 2 Kg 17:17; 23:10; 2 Ch 33:6; Ps 106:38; Je 7:31; Ez 16:20; etc). (106)

Jeremiah (32:34-35) in particular thundered angrily against the foul practice of offering children as a burnt sacrifice to Moloch, who was the tutelary deity of the people of Ammon, and essentially, identical with Chemosh of the Moabites. Fire-gods appear to have been common to all the Canaanite, Syrian and Arab tribes, who worshipped the destructive element under an outward symbol, with the most inhuman rites. (107)

Moloch was made of hollow brass. A fire was kindled in his belly and when he was red hot a child was placed on his outstretched and upraised arms, to roll down through a hole into the flames and be consumed.

---

(106) Awful as it is to read of parents treating their children with such cruelty, I wonder if God did not find more pleasure in those people than he does in many today, for two reasons: *(1)* at least those people had an awareness of sin, a sense of their need for heaven's pardon, a heart to pray, even if it was to Moloch and not Yahweh, in contrast with the heedless indifference to God and utter earth-bound materialism of our time; and *(2)* the terrible toll that is being taken of young life today through *(a)* the holocaust of abortion on demand, and *(b)* the growing number of single-parent families. Recent surveys have demonstrated how deeply children are hurt by family breakdown, what fearful consequences develop in later life in people who were deliberately abandoned by one parent or the other in childhood. At the root of both problems (abortion and marital collapse) lies an ugly self-centredness, people whose highest concern is nothing beyond their own comfort and happiness. The cries of children in the 20th century must sound as dreadful in the ears of God as did the sobs of the little ones perishing in the arms of fiery Moloch of old.

(107) Smith's Bible Dictionary, *in. loc.*

In order to drown the screams of the victims, flutes were played, and drums were loudly beaten. The mothers of the shrieking babies were required to stand by without tears or sobs, to give an impression of the voluntary character of their offering. (108)

On a more humane scale, the universal urge toward outer cleanliness and beauty is an echo of a deep internal desire for holiness. Even gangsters prefer to live in beautiful mansions, kept meticulously clean, and adorned with all manner of lovely artifacts, paintings, and sculptures! A newly washed car seems to run more sweetly than a dirty one! We keep our rubbish dumps as far out of sight as possible!

Yet nothing satisfies. The eye craves better things to see, the ear more charming things to hear, and the mouth sweeter things to eat, but their hunger remains unrequited (Ecc 1:8). How then can we be holy? How can this restless yearning find rest?

The glory of the gospel is this, that it requires us to put all our trust in just two things –

THE WORK OF CHRIST

> *Even when you were dead because of your offenses and the uncircumcision of your flesh, God made you alive with Christ when he forgave us all of our offenses, having erased the charges that were brought against us with their decrees that were hostile to us. He took those charges away when he nailed them to the cross. (Cl 2:13-14, ISV)*

By the "work" of Christ I mean his two fold work –

---

(108) International Standard Bible Encyclopedia, *in loc*. James A. Michener's 1964 novel The Source contains a vivid description of one such sacrifice.

- at **_Calvary_** as our *Sacrifice*, where he made full atonement for all our wrongdoing; and
- at the **_Throne_**, as our *High Priest*, where he makes unbroken intercession on our behalf (He 7:25), thus becoming the source of *"uttermost"* salvation to all who trust in him.

The Greek adjective translated *uttermost* is remarkably rich. It may be applied to the *uttermost* –

- **_time_** – that is, we gain a salvation in Christ that will endure through eternity; not all the vicissitudes of time can shake its foundations.
- **_position_** – as his Royal Priests we are exalted in Christ to the right hand of the Majesty on high, where we share his authority and dominion.
- **_character_** – the salvation of God reaches into and cleanses and changes us in the depths of our being, and reshapes us into the likeness of Christ
- **_kingdom_** – that is, we are assured of persevering until Christ returns and the ultimate plan of God begins to unfold.

THE WORD OF GOD

In 1543 John Heywood wrote a book called *The Three Ps*, about a Palmer, a Pardoner, a Poticiary, and a Peddler. [109] In one scene the four men argue about who can tell the greatest lie. The Palmer declared that he had never seen a woman out of patience. The others at once surrendered, reckoning that they could never better that falsehood!

---

(109) *Palmer* – a Pilgrim (who often carried palm leaves). *Pardoner* – a priest who sold indulgences. *Poticiary* – a travelling drug seller. *Peddler* – a travelling merchant, or tinker.

Well, I suppose that there are times when we are all good liars, but there is one utterly trustworthy source of indelible truth – the Bible. Yet sometimes, I admit, the promise does seem too good to be true. Thus, scripture declares that we are already made the righteousness of God in Christ; nothing we can do can either add to nor detract from that completed work. Against every natural instinct, we are called simply to appropriate the promise of God, and to rejoice in it.

For example, look at the following passage, where Paul lists many extraordinary achievements and sufferings upon which he might have based a claim of personal righteousness; but he rejects them all –

> *In every way we demonstrate that we are God's servants by tremendous endurance in the midst of difficulties, hardships, and calamities; in beatings, imprisonments, and riots; in hard work, sleepless nights, and hunger; with purity, knowledge, patience, and kindness; with the Holy Spirit, genuine love, truthful speech, and divine power; through the weapons of righteousness in the right and left hands. (2 Co 6:4-7, ISV)*

He does not hesitate to claim his privations and virtues as worthy commendations of his ministry to the church; but when he is about to approach the throne of God he suggests that he will offer nothing to the Father except the righteousness of Christ, filling up his left hand and his right hand, so that no room remains to hold *anything* else (vs 7b). He has and wants no other plea but Christ to commend him to God.

The same idea is stated clearly in this passage –

> *We know that people don't receive God's approval because of some strenuous effort to obey a set of rules, but only by believing in Jesus Christ. <u>Even we apostles are content to</u>*

> *<u>believe in Jesus Christ</u>, so that we might gain God's approval by faith in Christ and not because of our own efforts. No one will ever gain God's approval by struggling to attain merit through an abundance of good works. (Ga 2:16)*

If Paul reckoned that not all his pains and labours would gain him so much as one grain of righteousness in God's sight, what chance do you and I have? We had better believe in Christ, trust the grace of God, stand on the promise, and be done with it!

But this does raise the question: "How do you know that you are saved?" Do you base your claim upon some good thing you have done, some great sacrifice you have made, or some religious experience you have had? Many people do just that! Yet how absurd are all such attempts.

GK Chesterton's fictional detective Father Brown in one place explains the secret of his seemingly uncanny ability to solve the mystery of some dreadful crime. He said that he turned himself into the criminal by stripping away from himself all the veneer of his training and culture until he reached the level of the person who could do such a deed. Then he was able to think like that person and follow the steps he or she took toward the crime. Father Brown explained it this way –

> I wait until I know I am inside the murderer, thinking his thoughts, wrestling with his passions; till I have bent myself into the posture of his hunched and peering hatred; till I see the world with his bloodshot and squinting eyes, looking between the blinkers of his half-witted concentration; looking up the short and sharp perspective of a straight road to a pool of blood, Till I am really a murderer. ... No man's really any good till he knows how bad he is or might be; till he's realised exactly

> how much right he has to all his snobbery, and sneering, and talking about "criminals", as if they were apes in a forest ten thousand miles away; till he's got rid of all the dirty self-deception of talking about low types and deficient skulls; till he's squeezed out of his soul the last drop of the oil of the Pharisee ... (110)

How true that is! We think we are nice people mostly because we have never been truly honest with ourselves. But anyone who compels himself to the severe introspection practised by Father Brown will discover that, had he born in another place, or another time, or had he been raised under different influences, has within himself a potential to commit almost any crime, no matter how hideous. We are all skilled at cloaking ourselves with the camouflage of the Pharisee. Nothing less than union with Christ can finally eradicate that inner evil and make us truly children of God, full of his love.

It means that without God shows us undeserved mercy, we are altogether undone. So that our song should always and only be –

> My hope is built on nothing less
>   Than Jesus' blood and righteousness;
> I dare not trust the sweetest frame,
>   But wholly lean on Jesus' name! [111]

---

(110) From the fictional foreword to the collection, <u>The Secret of Father Brown</u> (1927) by GK Chesterton; cited in <u>The Best of Father Brown</u>, selected and edited by HRF Keating; Everyman's Library; JM Dent and Sons Ltd, London, 1987; pg. 6, 7.

(111) *On Christ the Solid Rock I Stand,* by Edward Mote (1797-1874) who was an English Baptist pastor. After many years of faithful service at the one church, it is said that the congregation lovingly offered to give him the title to the building, upon which he replied, "I do not want the chapel, I only want the pulpit; and when I cease to preach Christ, then turn me out of that!"

THE RESURRECTION OF CHRIST – SUFFICIENT FOR YOUR VICTORY

The world has never heard any better news than this: *"Christ is risen!"* To us who believe, it declares that death and the devil are both utterly defeated, and that we are utterly victorious! On the strength of it, Paul urges us to live in the energy of Christ's resurrection. This is a major key to overcoming the tug of our fallen nature and discovering a new and victorious life in Christ –

> *If the Spirit of him that raised up Jesus from the dead dwell in you, he that raised up Christ from the dead shall also quicken your mortal bodies by his Spirit that dwelleth in you. (Ro 8:11, KJV)*

How can we do this? In two ways –

BE FILLED WITH THE SPIRIT (VS. 12-16)

It is the peculiar task of the Holy Spirit to impart to us in an ever-increasing measure the resurrection life of Christ. One way he does this is through the supernatural channel of *glossolalia* (of which the Aramaic diminutive *"Abba!"* seems to be a synonym, an epitome of what the glossolalist is saying, or of how the Father hears glossolalia – as a loving parent hears the cry of an infant).

Glossolalia, too, is like an echo of the earthquake that shook open the tomb of Jesus; it is a channel through which his resurrection life can flow into and through the life of the Spirit-filled believer. But note that the manner in which the language is spoken is altogether under the control of the speaker (1 Co 14:14-15); which means that it will have no value unless it is spoken with fervour, love, faith, strength, joy (1 Co 13:1).

TAKE UP THE CROSS (VS. 17-18)

What a paradox – we must die in order to live!

But in the economy of God there has never been any resurrection unless the cross came first. Note how Paul exemplifies both cross and crown –

- on the one hand, what zeal, what faith, what victory, miracles, authority, and sheer dynamic *life* we observe in the great apostle
- yet on the other, what suffering, what sacrifice, what endurance and toil, what *dying* (see Ro 8:35-36; 1 Co 4:9-13; 2 Co 4:8-12; 6:4-10; 11:23-27).

Paul demonstrated in himself the principle that as surely as there is no death without first there is life, so there is no life without first there is death (Jn 12:23-26).

Does that mean that you and I cannot truly experience the love and life of Christ unless we suffer as Paul did? No, for God demands from each one of us a level of obedience that to us will be like the crucifixion of our flesh. This will take a different shape for each believer – perhaps a burden of prayer for one, or of persecution for another; or a burden of service, or giving, or love, or ministry, and so on. Hence Jesus said: *"Take up your (own) cross, and follow me"* (Mt 16:24-25).

CONCLUSION

In the 16th century Richard Whiting, the last abbot of Glastonbury, tried to turn King Henry VIII aside from his intention of commandeering his abbey. He took the title deeds of 12 estates, concealed them in a large Christmas pie, and commissioned his chief steward, John Horner, to deliver the pie safely to the king. According to legend, Horner somehow discovered what the pie contained, lifted its crust, and pulled out the deed to an estate known as *Mells Park*.

The abbot's ploy failed. He still lost his abbey; but the Horner family gained a fine estate! [112]

The story inspired the familiar nursery rhyme –

> Little Jack Horner sat in his corner
> Eating his Christmas pie;
> He put in his thumb and pulled out a plum,
> And said, "What a good boy am I!"

It may be stretching the usefulness of the rhyme a little, yet I hope that is what you will do with this magnificent revelation of the all-sufficiency of Christ. There is no other way to true goodness than to savour Christ, to become wholly his as he is wholly yours. Christ is enough. You need no other. No other can equal him. Grasp him by faith, until you can sing with Paul, *"As surely as all the fulness of the Godhead dwells bodily in Christ, so surely does all the fulness of Christ dwell bodily in me!"*

There indeed is transformation; there is joy; there is heaven on earth; there alone is Paradise to come; there is your heavenly mansion, an indestructible estate, and an eternity of laughing worship and service of the King.

---

(112) While records show that Thomas Horner did indeed become the owner of the manor, his descendants and subsequent owners of Mells Manor have claimed that the legend is somewhat libellous, and that the property was purchased legally in 1543. The Horner family kept the mansion until the death of Sir John Horner, the last of the name, in 1927 (http://webapp1.somerset.gov.uk/her/details.asp?prn=23827).

Chapter Nineteen

LIFE IN CHRIST

> *If when we were enemies, we were reconciled to God by the death of his Son; much more, being reconciled, we shall be **saved by his life** (Ro 5:10).*

People are often deterred from embarking upon Christian life because of a fear that they will not be able to live it out; or that they will backslide. They dread finding themselves on the day of Judgment in a worse position than they would have been if they had never tried to be Christians.

They are, of course, quite correct, for no one can live a Christian life!

Only one Man has ever been able to do so, and that was Jesus.

But our text shows us that Christ, having reconciled us to God by his **death** (thus giving us eternal life in heaven), now wants to save us on earth (that is, give us daily victory) by his **life**. I mean that

- he died to save us from what we have done; that is, the Cross is adequate to rescue us from all the guilt of our past sin; but

- he lives to save us from what we are; that is, he wants to supplant our natural life with his own resurrection life.

So the Lord calls us to a life of righteousness; but since we cannot possibly fulfil that call unaided, he wants to subdue our mortal life beneath his eternal life, and to live through us himself.

Here are four steps we should take so that Christ may be fully alive in us each day –

MAKE YOURSELF COMPLETELY DEPENDENT UPON CHRIST

See how Jesus himself consistently acted on the premise that without the Father he could do nothing –

> *Jesus said to the Jews, "I can guarantee this truth: The Son cannot do anything on his own. He can do only what he sees the Father doing. Indeed, the Son does exactly what the Father does. ... The Father who has life sent me, and I live because of the Father." (Jn 5:19; 6:57, GW)*

If that was true of *Christ*, how can *we* hope to live independently of his indwelling grace and strength? So Christ made his own experience the basis of his promise of life to his disciples. Just as the Father had dwelt in and acted through him, so now he will do the same for those who trust him –

> *I am the vine. You are the branches. Those who live in me while I live in them will produce a lot of fruit. But you can't produce anything without me. (Jn 15:5, GW)*

So we are to be as dependent upon Christ as a branch is to a vine; or, to change the simile, as dependent as your arm is to your body; or, even better, as the body itself is to the head.

Think of a chicken able still to run around for a time, even after its head has been cut off! Some Christians are like that – running around, seemingly active and alive, yet it is all a sham, for they have cut themselves off from the Head.

SET YOURSELF TO OBEY THE FATHER'S WILL

How obedient was Jesus to his Father's command?

> *Jesus told them, "When you have lifted up the Son of Man, then you'll know that I am the one and that <u>I can't do anything on my own</u>. Instead, <u>I speak as the Father taught me</u>. ... (Jn 8:28-29, GW)*

His obedience was perfect and absolute. He never reckoned it possible that he would do either more nor less than the Father asked of him; it was unthinkable that he would defy the Father's purpose. Had he not come to fulfil that purpose? As scripture had foretold –

> *Here I am, O Lord. Just as it is written of me in your Book, "I have come, O God, to do your will" (He 10:7,9, quoting Ps 40:7).*

Which brings us to a vital question. How far are you willing to obey God? Do you have any reservations, any limits, any exclusions?

This issue must be faced by every believer, and settled once and for all. In fact, we should all test ourselves on this question from time to time, assessing whether or not we have fallen away from full obedience. Ask yourself, "Am I still truly listening for the Father's voice as once I did?"

Absolute surrender is demanded from us all. As Hudson Taylor used to say, "Christ will not be Lord at all if he is not Lord of all." To which he added –

> I used to ask God to help me. Then I asked if I might help him. I ended up by asking him to do his work through me. (113)

Without such a full yielding to the Lord, there can be no true experience of the indwelling and empowering life of Christ.

BECOME AVAILABLE TO ALL THAT GOD HAS FOR YOU

How much of God do you want? How much of his blessing? How much of his promise?

In the end, it must be **everything** or it will be **nothing.** We are not free to pick and choose among the promises and commands of God. We cannot embrace one promise but disdain another; we cannot express willingness to obey God here, but not there; we cannot desire *this* blessing from the Father while rejecting *that*.

Think for a moment – how long will a marriage last if one spouse says to the other: "I want only some of your love, some of your care, some of your strength"?

How absurd! Two people who love each other want all of each other; they cannot be content either with a half-given or half-received love; it must be all or nothing, else their protestations of true love are a mockery.

There are two powerful elements in a long-lasting marital union; two things that probably express the greatest gifts that the partners expect from and can give to each other –

---

(113) I have been unable to locate the source of either of those quotes. The first saying also has been attributed to other people, among them AW Tozer, SM Zwemer, John Calvin, etc. It is often cited as, "If Christ is not Lord of all then he is not Lord at all."

- ***There is the gift that the <u>husband</u> gives to his wife*** – that is, a total <u>commitment</u> both to the permanency of the union and to the happiness of his wife.

A good wife wants to know that her husband truly meant it when he vowed to "cleave only unto her, for better for worse, for richer for poorer, in sickness and in health, to love and to cherish, till death us do part." She is entitled to the security that comes from knowing her husband is committed to the permanency of their marriage. Her love for him will flourish best in an environment of knowing that his deepest desire is not to extract happiness *from* her, but rather to bring it *to* her. When he fulfils these things, a godly husband makes himself a type-picture of God; he becomes to his wife what Christ wishes to be to the Church.

- ***There is the gift that the <u>wife</u> gives to her husband*** – that is, a loving <u>abandonment</u> to the desire of her husband, knowing that she can trust him utterly to do her no harm.

There is perhaps no more sacred, nor more prized gift that a virtuous woman can give to her husband than an uninhibited surrender to his love, a yielding that he knows she would rather die than offer to any other man. In this she shows both the depth of her love for him, and the degree of her trust in him. Thus she becomes a picture of the relationship the Church should have with Christ.

There is no limit to what God can do for you, through you, with you, if you are available to everything he has for you!

CONFRONT EVERY SITUATION IN THE ADEQUACY OF CHRIST

Just as we by faith have appropriated the efficacy of what Christ has ***done*** for us, so we must also by faith seize the adequacy of what Christ is ***in*** us.

In every new situation in life, develop the habit, before you confront it, of pausing for a moment, long enough to unite yourself deliberately with Christ.

The scripture speaks truly: you **can** do all things in Christ, if you allow him to infuse you with his own indestructible life! (Ph 4:13)

LAST WORDS

How difficult it is to end this book! I understand now what John was feeling when he wrote –

> *There are many other things that Jesus did. If all of them were to be written, I suppose that the whole world would not be big enough to hold all the books that would be written! (21:25).*

Christ is so splendid that I feel, despite all the pages that lie behind me, I have scarcely placed one foot in the shallow edge of the ocean of his glory and beauty. Which reminds me of a story told about St Augustine (354-430), one of the truly great Fathers of the church. He devoted much labour and thought to the mystery of the Trinity, and wrote a major treatise on the theme, *De Trinitatis*, while confessing that the task of reducing the glory of the Deity to human words was impossible. The legend says that while he was meditating on his mighty subject, he had a vision of a child trying to empty the ocean by using a shell to scoop it up and pour it into a hole in the sand. When he remarked on the futility of trying to put the sea into such a small space, the child rebuked him, "My toils are less foolish than yours, who hope to comprehend the Trinity in the pages of your small book!" (114)

Well, my book too is a little hole, and it is a fantastic notion to suppose that it contains anything more than a few dribbles of muddied truth about the supernal radiance and endless splendour of Christ and of the Godhead.

However, the frailties of flesh and the exigencies of time demand that we end our adventure when it seems hardly to have begun. But let us at least step out of the water with two pearls in hand; pearls that shine with the lustre of Jesus.

The first is another selection from the exquisite poetry of Gerard Manley Hopkins. It portrays what Christ's incarnation should mean to you in your inner self. The second is a 5th century poem, which portrays how the incarnation should affect your view of the world outside of yourself.

> May God give us eyes to see Jesus.
> "I am all at once what Christ is,
> since he was what I am, and
> This Jack, joke, poor potsherd, patch,
> matchwood, immortal diamond,
> Is immortal diamond." (115)

Christ with me, Christ before me, Christ behind me,
Christ in me, Christ beneath me, Christ above me,
Christ on my right, Christ on my left,
Christ when I lie down,
Christ when I sit down,
Christ when I arise,
Christ in the heart of every man who thinks of me,

---

(114) <u>Dictionary of Christian Lore and Legend</u>, ed. JCJ Metford; Thames and Hudson Ltd, London; 1983; *in loc.*

(115) *Poem #72*, last lines.

Christ in the mouth of every one who speaks of me,
Christ in the eye of every one who sees me,
Christ in every ear that hears me.

I arise today
Through a mighty strength, the invocation of the Trinity,
Through belief in the threeness,
Through confession of the oneness
Of the Creator of Creation. [116]

---

(116) From *The Lorica*, attributed to St Patrick (*circa* 377), last two stanzas; tr. by Kuno Meyer. "Lorica" is a Latin word that means a piece of body armour, often a breastplate. The word also sometimes means a mystical garment, designed to protect the wearer from harm or illness. The poem can be found online in a number of different versions. It has also been adapted as a hymn, which begins, *"I bind unto myself today / The strong Name of the Trinity, / By invocation of the same / The Three in One and One in Three."*

ADDENDUM

THE CATHOLIC VIEW

This explanation of the Catholic viewpoint on Mary is drawn from a number of Catholic writings, mainly scholarly in character (that is, not popular devotional works), and all bearing the "Nihil Obstat" (= "nothing hinders" = approval by the official censor) and "Imprimatur" (= "let it be printed" = official approval to publish a book.) My intention is simply to state the Catholic position without much comment, and I hope that the necessary brevity of the statement will not compromise its fairness and accuracy. Should any Catholic reader feel that I have misrepresented the teaching of the Church I would be grateful for appropriate correction.

THE IMMACULATE CONCEPTION OF MARY

In response to a long tradition within the Church, Pope Pius IX, in 1854, promulgated the bull *Ineffabilis Deus*, in which he wrote –

> We declare, pronounce, and define – the doctrine that maintains that the most Blessed Virgin Mary in the first instant of her conception, by a unique grace and privilege of the omnipotent God and in consideration of the merits of Christ Jesus the Saviour of the human race, was preserved free from all stain of original sin, is a doctrine revealed by God and therefore must be firmly and constantly held by all the faithful.

The doctrine means – by an act of God at the conception of Mary, both the stain of original sin and the active principle of sin were excluded from her; she was then able to live free of sin, possessing a righteousness marked by sanctity, innocence, and justice. However, this did not prevent her from being subject to such temporal and physical effects of the Fall as sickness, pain, death; hence her "sinlessness" was not of the same order as that of Christ.

THE PERPETUAL VIRGINITY OF MARY

It is evident that Mary's betrothal to Joseph shows that her first intention was to enter into a normal relationship with him after their marriage. However, Catholics assert that after the Annunciation, Mary vowed upon herself perpetual virginity, so that although Joseph married her, he did so simply to provide care and protection for her and for the Infant, being content not to have intercourse with her.

Objections to this concept are raised on the basis of

- *Matthew 1:25*. The word "until" is reckoned to indicate that Mary did have intercourse with Joseph after the birth of Jesus. To which Catholics respond that such a reading may be suggested by our English translations, but it is absent from the Greek particle (*heos*) used by Matthew. The Greek text does not contain the implication found in the English translation; it is simply a statement of the fact that Mary was still a virgin at the time of Jesus' birth. Protestants usually say that the Greek text is open to either reading, and that the matter cannot be finally proved one way or the other.

- The *"brothers and sisters"* of Christ referred to in the NT surely prove that Mary had children by Joseph (Mt 12:46-50; Mk 6:3; etc).

To which Catholics answer –

- The Greek words used in these passages, especially within a Semitic community, just as readily mean "cousins" as "brothers" or "sisters".

- Two of Jesus' brethren were certainly sons of a Mary different from Mary his mother (Mk 6:3; 15:40).

- Jesus' act (Jn 19:26-27) of giving Mary into the keeping of John remains inexplicable if Jesus had brothers and sisters.

- The designation of Jesus as "the" son of Mary (Mk 6:3) indicates that he was Mary's only child.

- The fact that Mary was able to go on a 14-day pilgrimage to Jerusalem when Jesus was 12 years old (Lu 2:41-52), indicates that there were no younger children in the family at that time.

- "If Mary had had other children after this pilgrimage, these would not have reached the age of 20 by the time Jesus began his public life, and would never have been able to behave towards their elder brother in such a free and easy manner ... (In) *Mark 3:21, 31-35* and *John 7:2-5* ... they appear to treat him almost as a guardian treats his ward" (Bauer).

- The conclusions must be that these *"brothers and sisters"* were either cousins of Jesus, or perhaps the children of Joseph by an earlier marriage (a view supported by an ancient tradition in the church).

Some Protestants would agree with, or at least have no strong objection to, those arguments. Others say that the most natural reading of the texts points to several natural siblings of Jesus (four actual brothers and an unknown number of sisters). Apart from dogma, the matter does not seem to impinge upon our salvation either one way or the other

The tradition that Mary was, is, and ever will be a virgin dates from the early church Fathers, who argued that for Mary to have had children conceived in sin would be irreverent, betraying lack of real thought about the issues involved. Protestants feel, however, that such ascetic scruples are not endorsed in scripture, and are no basis upon which to build significant doctrine. (117)

It is true that Pope Siricius wrote (AD 392) – " ... the Lord Jesus would not have chosen to be born of a virgin if he had judged that she would be so incontinent as to taint the birthplace of the body of the Lord, the home of the eternal king, with the seed of human intercourse." It is also true that such sentiments betray a cultural setting in which celibacy was extolled as more virtuous than the married state (an idea that few Christians today would find acceptable).

Nonetheless, the opinions of the Fathers did reflect a deep instinctive feeling in the hearts of multitudes of Christians. The idea that Mary kept her virginity before, during, and after the birth of Christ seemed so "right" that it early found almost universal acceptance in the church, and was later confirmed by serious thinking theologians. Such deep-rooted, ancient, and profoundly held convictions should not be lightly discarded. However, they will plainly have a stronger or weaker force, depending upon the background and mindset of those who contemplate them. Protestants generally do not find them compelling, and few Protestants would feel obliged to insist upon Mary's perpetual virginity, especially since (apart from the references to Jesus' "brothers and sisters") there is scant biblical evidence one way or the other. . (118)

---

(117) Not all the Fathers agreed with such notions. For example, Clement of Alexandria (Miscellanies, Bk. VII, Ch 16) records that "many even down to our own time (*circa* 200) regard Mary, on account of the birth of her child, as having been in the puerperal state." Clement himself, however, seems to have believed in her continuing virginity.

(118) In the 6th cent. a Roman nobleman, Cassiodorus (died *c.* 560), translated into Latin the works of the early 3rd. cent. bishop Clement of Alexandria. One piece that remains contains a series of comments on the *Letter of Jude*, which begin thus – "Jude,

(continued on next page)

THE ASSUMPTION OF MARY

The tradition of the Assumption of Mary developed much later in the church than the tradition of her sinlessness and unbroken virginity. Nonetheless, traces of this tradition exist in some writings from as early as the 4th century, and by the end of the 6th century belief in Mary's bodily assumption was firmly established.

Many theologians spoke in support of the tradition, arguing for it on the basis of its intrinsic reasonableness; namely, the improbability of God allowing the body in which his Son had once dwelt to see corruption. This, Catholics claim, is a logical, if not inevitable, extension of the idea found in *Acts 2:27*.

Pope Pius XII, in 1950, pronounced the Assumption of Mary as an article of faith for all true Catholics. He said –

> We proclaim, declare and define it to be a dogma revealed by God that the immaculate mother of God, Mary ever-virgin, when the course of her earthly life was finished, was taken up body and soul into the glory of heaven.

Similarly –

> The unique privilege of being assumed bodily into heaven, stems from her unique privilege of being the Mother of God conceived free of

---

(continued from previous page)

> who wrote the Catholic Epistle, the brother of the sons of Joseph, and very religious, whilst knowing the near relationship of the Lord, yet did not say that he himself was his brother. But what said he? 'Jude, a servant of Jesus Christ,' – of him as Lord; but 'the brother of James.' For this is true; he was his brother, (the son) of Joseph." This appears to be confirmation of an early belief that Jesus was an actual brother of Jude.

original sin. In her assumption she is preserved free from the decay of death. Furthermore, our Christian hope lies in the prospect of sharing in the resurrection of Jesus. Mary the mother of Jesus is the first to share in his resurrection. In doing so she becomes a living model of the Church in its future destiny of unity with the risen Christ. Mary is, in other words, a living model ... of the new humanity born of her Son, the new Adam, who brought eternal life to all who believe in him. [119]

In this context, the Fathers saw Mary as a figure of the church, the new Eve; and they understood *John 19:26-27* as an acted parable of the spiritual motherhood of Mary toward all the faithful, expressed through the church. This is echoed in a statement from the documents of the Second Vatican Council – "In the bodily and spiritual glory which she possesses in heaven, the Mother of Jesus continues in this present world as the image and first flowering of the Church as she is to be perfected in the world to come." [120]

THE WORSHIP OF MARY

It should be noted that Catholics deny that they "worship" Mary. They use three Latin words to define three levels of worship – *latria* = the worship due to God alone; *hyperdulia* = high veneration due to Mary; *dulia* = the special honour due to the saints. Catholics who are careful in their practice would never accord Mary the same level of reverence as they give to Christ, for they realise that it is Mary who gains her favoured position from Christ, not vice versa.

---

(119) Your Faith and You; James Finley and Michael Pennock; Ave Maria Press, Notre Dame, Ind., USA; 1978; pg. 239,240.

(120) Constitution of the Church; *Lumen Gentium 68*; quoted by Finley and Pennock, *ibid.*

Nonetheless, they do maintain that exalted honour should be given to Mary as *theotokos* = "God-bearer", or (based on the parallel Latin word) "Mother-of-God." In this honour she stands alone among human kind, and scripture says that all generations will call her *"blessed."* The reverential regard in which Catholics hold Mary is warranted by the high favour granted her by God. Their belief that she can mediate favour to the church is based on the words of the angel – *"Rejoice, O highly favoured daughter! The Lord is with you. Blessed are you among women"* (Lu 1:28, NAB).

> Because the verb ("highly favoured", literally, "grace-endowed") is also a participle, Mary is shown to have been chosen for a long time past; God's full flow of favour has already been concentrating upon her ... Mary, more than any other human being in the Bible, is the recipient of the most impressive salutations – *Luke 1:28,30,35,42-49; 2:19 f, 34* ... In her, more than in anyone else, God's messianic fulfilment is achieved. As such, she has received more – from and through God's anticipation of Jesus' redemptive work – than anyone else in the OT or NT. (*The Jerome Biblical Commentary*, in loc).

> Christian tradition has concluded from the greeting of the angel and the unique destiny reserved for Mary that she was given grace in a special measure and united with God in such a way that she was "full of grace" (the Latin translation of Lu 1:28). As early as the patristic age the greeting of the angel was understood in this way to signify that Mary was filled with grace (Bauer, *Encyclopedia of Biblical Theology*).

THE THREEFOLD FOUNDATION OF THESE DOGMAS

Catholic teaching about Mary rests upon three sources –

SCRIPTURE

The Biblical foundation for Catholic belief about Mary is *first*, the various NT references to her; *second*, OT references which are closely associated with her, viz *Genesis 3:15; Isaiah 7:14*; *third*, OT references which are symbolic of her, e.g. *Psalm 45:12-17*.

Catholics readily allow that none of those references plainly support any of the dogmas outlined above; but neither does the Bible provide any denial of those dogmas. On the contrary, Catholics insist that all the various dogmas about Mary may be reasonably inferred, or developed, from the biblical data. Hence the Fathers

> taught that, as the first woman might have foiled the tempter and did not, so, had Mary been disobedient or unbelieving of Gabriel's message, the Divine Economy would have been frustrated. And certainly the parallel between *"the Mother of all living"* (Eve) and the Mother of the Redeemer may be gathered from a comparison of the first chapters of Scripture with the last ... Tertullian (c 200) says that, whereas Eve believed the Serpent, and Mary believed Gabriel, "what Eve failed in believing, Mary by believing hath blotted out."

> St Irenaeus (c180) speaks more explicitly – "As Eve," he says, "was seduced by the angel's speech so as to flee God, having trangressed his word, so also Mary by an angel's speech was evangelised so as to contain God, being obedient to his word. And as the one was seduced to flee God, so the other was

persuaded to body God, that the Virgin Mary might become the Advocate (Paraclete) of the Virgin Eve, that as mankind has been bound to death through a virgin, through a virgin it may be saved – virginal disobedience by virginal obedience, the balance being made equal." And elsewhere, "As Eve ... became the cause of death to herself and to all mankind, so Mary ... became cause of salvation both to herself and to all mankind ... for what the virgin Eve tied through unbelief, that the Virgin Mary unties through faith." This becomes the received doctrine in the Post-Nicene Church. [121]

In this manner, and over many centuries, Catholic dogma about Mary was developed out of propositions that were reckoned to be implied in scripture.

REASON

Catholics argue that the Marian dogmas are inescapable when due thought is given to the nature of the virginal conception and birth of the Son of God through Mary. If she was "the mother of *Jesus*" (Jn 2:1), and if Jesus was God, then she was "the mother of *God*" – and from this fact all the other teachings of the church about Mary flow irresistibly.

TRADITION

There is no certain historical data about the time or place of Mary's birth, her age, her parentage, her later life, or her death. However, the traditions about her, and the devotional

---

(121) Cardinal J.H. Newman, in his famous <u>Essay on the Development of Christian Doctrine</u>. The above selection is from the first edition of the essay, published in 1854, before Newman's conversion to Catholicism. It is taken from a Penguin Classic, published in 1974, pg. 390. This book, of course, does not carry any Catholic authorisation.

attitudes toward her are very ancient indeed, with the first records of these things appearing within a hundred years or so of the death of the apostles.

For example, *The Book Of James* (which dates back to c. 150, when people were still alive who had personally known members of the holy family and the apostles) is the source of the tradition that Mary's parents were Joachim and Anna, and that miracles attended her birth, her childhood, and her eventual marriage to Joseph. The same book attests to Mary's perpetual virginity, and claims that the "brethren of Jesus" were the children of Joseph by a previous marriage.

Catholics argue that such early and widespread traditions cannot be ignored; and that the Church has a right and a duty to determine which of them should be accepted as fact.

SUMMARY

A distinction must be made between those dogmas about Mary which are actually and officially promulgated by the Church, and the various popular views (some of them extreme) which are held by Catholic people. Not all that Catholic people write and say about Mary is approved by the Church.

A cautious approach to these matters is shown by many serious thinkers –

> Any theological reflections about Mary must begin from scripture. The Bible provides us with some direct information about Mary, while other conclusions can be deduced indirectly from them. Hence it is that the church, with the help of tradition, has deduced from scripture more than is warranted by historical and critical exegesis, by using a kind of interpretation which is not easy to define with any exactitude. There are some theologians who go even further and develop

doctrine about Mary for which scripture offers no justification apart from the most general principles. (122)

A Roman Catholic must accept the two dogmas (the Immaculate Conception, and the Assumption of Mary) as true upon the authority of the teaching Church, but he does not have to hold that the dogmas are derived from a chain of historical information. There is no evidence that Mary (or anyone else in NT times) knew that she was conceived free of original sin, especially since the concept of original sin did not fully exist in the first century.

The dogma is not based upon information passed down by Mary or by the apostles; it is based on the Church's insight that the sinlessness of Jesus should have affected his origins, and hence his mother, as well. Nor does a Catholic have to think that the people gathered for her funeral saw Mary assumed into heaven – there is no reliable historical tradition to that effect, and the dogma does not even specify that Mary died. Once again the doctrine stems from the Church's insight about the application of the fruits of redemption to the leading Christian disciple – Mary has gone before us, anticipating our common fate. (123)

---

(122) Encyclopedia of Biblical Theology; ed J.B. Bauer; Sheed and Ward, London, 1970; pg. 561.

(123) R.E. Brown, Crises Facing The Church; Darton, Longman & Todd, London; 1975; footnote on pg. 105. Dr Brown, a leading Catholic biblical scholar, was appointed by Pope Paul VI to the Roman Pontifical Commission. His book is a penetrating
(continued on next page)

Protestants of course, with their stern adherence to *sola scriptura*, find such arguments far from compelling.

VERY LAST WORDS

Toward the end of his great book of Hebrew wisdom, Sirach wrote –

> Out of my learning and understanding, and from my very heart, I have written this book, pouring out wisdom like water from a fountain. Happy are those who make these things a deep concern, and who lay them to heart. They too will become wise, and if they also do them will be equal to anything that comes their way, for the light of the Lord will illuminate their path. (50:27-29)

I hope you will not think me arrogant if I lay claim to the same things (at least in part) for the two books I have now completed on *Emmanuel*. Yet having written so much, the task is not done, nor ever will be. For as Sirach again declared long ago (43:27) –

> No matter how much I say,
> I cannot reach an end;
> So the sum of all my words must be,
> "He is the All!"

(continued from previous page)

examination of several issues that are still of vital concern to both Catholics and Protestants – especially the exploration of ways of building bridges across the great divides in Christendom.

BIBLIOGRAPHY

BOOKS

Banner of Truth Trust; *Systematic Theology;* London, 1976.

_____ *A Body Of Divinity*; 1958.

Barnes, A. *Notes on the New Testament.* Kregel Publications: Grand Rapids, Michigan, 1966

Bauer, J. B. *Encyclopedia of Biblical Theology.* Sheed and Ward: London, 1970.

Bettenson, Henry, *Documents of the Christian Church.* Oxford University Press: London, 1975.

Brown, R. E. *Crises Facing The Church.* Darton, Longman & Todd: London, 1975.

Chesterton G.K., selected and edited by H. R. F. Keating. *The Best of Father Brown.* Everyman's Library, J.M. Dent and Sons Ltd: London, 1987.

Chafer, S. L. *Systematic Theology.* Dallas Seminary Press: Dallas, Texas, 1947.

Donaldson, J. and Roberts A., editors, *The Ante-Nicene Fathers.* Eerdman's Publishing Company: Grand Rapids, Michigan, 1978.

Douglas, J. D. General editor, *The New International Dictionary of the Christian Church.* Paternoster Press: 1974.

Eusebius, *Ecclesiastical History.* Baker Book House: Grand Rapids, Michigan, 1977

Finley, James, and Michael Pennock, *Your Faith and You.* Ave Maria Press: Notre Dame, Ind., USA, 1978.

Gifford, E. H. *The Incarnation.* Longmans, Green & Co: London, 1911.

Harrison E. F., editor in chief, *Baker's Dictionary of Theology.* Baker Book House: Grand Rapids, Michigan, 1978.

Hastings, James. Editor, *Dictionary of the New Testament*; *Vol. One.* reprinted by Baker Book House: Grand Rapids, Michigan, 1973.

Heywood, John, *The Three P's* (1543).

History of Christianity, A. Vol. One. Harper & Row: New York, 1975.

Hunter, C. F. *What A Christian Believes and Why.* Methodist Church: London, 1942.

Zondervan Pictorial Encyclopedia of the Bible Vol. 5. Zondervan Publishing House: Grand Rapids, Michigan, 1975.

Khayyam, Omar, tr. by Peter Avery and John-Heath-Stubbs. *The Ruba'iyat.* Penguin Classics, 1983.

Lewis, C. S. *On Scripture.* Hodder and Stoughton: London, 1980.

_____ *Surprised By Joy.* Fontana Books: London, 1975.

_____ *Mere Christianity.* Fontana Books: London, 1956.

Milford, Humphrey, *The Pageant of English Poetry.* Oxford University Press: London, NY, Toronto and Melbourne, 1914.

Newman, J. H. Essay; *The Development of Christian Doctrine* (1854). Penguin Classics, 1974.

Nicole, R. *Let The Earth Hear His Voice.* World Wide Publications: Minneapolis, Minnesota, 1975.

Opie, Iona & Peter, *The Oxford Dictionary of Nursery Rhymes.* Oxford University Press: 1985.

Orr, James, editor. *International Standard Bible Encyclopedia.* Howard-Severance Co: Chicago, 1915.

Strong, A. H. *Systematic Theology.* Pickering & Inglis: London, 1958.

Toon, Peter, (1833-1856). *The New Evangelical Theology.* Marshall, Morgan and Scott: London, 1969.

BIBLE COMMENTARIES

Anders, Max, editor. *Holman New Testament Commentary*. B & H Publishing Group: Nashville, Tennessee, 2004.

Barnes, Albert, (1798-1870) *Notes on the Bible*.

Bible Background Commentary. Intervarsity Press: Nottingham, U.K., 1993.

Calvin, John (1509-1564) *Calvin's Commentaries*.

Clarke, Adam (1715-1832) *Commentary on the Bible*.

College Press NIV Commentary, The. Joplin, Missouri, 1996.

Excell, Joseph S. and Spence-Jones, H. D. M. Editors, *The Pulpit Commentary*. 1881.

Gaebelein, Frank E. editor. *The Expositor's Bible Commentary*. Zondervan Publishers: Grand Rapids, Michigan.

Gill, John (1690-1771) *Exposition of the Entire Bible*.

Hawker, Robert, *The Poor Man's Commentary On The Whole Bible*. 1850.

Henry, Matthew (1662-1714), *Commentary On The Whole Bible*. Marshall, Morgan, and Scott: London, 1953 reprint.

Hodge, Charles (1797-1878).*A Commentary on Ephesians*. Intervarsity Press.

Interpreter's Bible, The. Abingdon Press: New York, 1952.

Ironside, H. A. *Expository Commentary* (1876-1951).

IVP New Testament Commentary Series, The. Intervarsity Press: Nottingham, UK.

Jamieson, R., A. Fausett and D. Brown. *A Commentary on the Old and New Testaments*. 1871.

Johnson B. W. *The People's New Testament Commentary*. 1891.

Macdonald, William, *Believer's Bible Commentary*. Thomas Nelson Publishers: 1989.

Nelson's New Illustrated Bible Commentary. Thomas Nelson Inc.,

New York, 1999.

New Testament Commentary, The. Baker's Publishing House: Grand Rapids, Michigan, 1987.

Poole, Matthew, *Matthew Poole's Commentary.* 1685

Preacher's Commentary, The. Word Inc., Nashville, Tennessee, 1992.

Preacher's Outline and Sermon Bible. Word Search Corporation: Nashville, Tennessee, 2010.

Robertson A. T. *Word Pictures in the New Testament;* 1933.

Stern, David H. *Jewish New Testament Commentary.* Jewish New Testament Publications Inc: Clarksville, Maryland; 1982.

Trapp, John, *Commentary On The Old And New Testaments* (1601-1669).

Vincent, Marvin R. *Vincent's Word Studies.* 1886

Walvoord, John and Zuck, Roy,*The Bible Knowledge Commentary.* Cook Communications: Colorado Springs, Colorado, 1989.

Wesley, John, *Explanatory Notes on the Whole Bible* (1703-1791).

Wiersbe, Warren W. *Wiersbe's Expository Outlines.* Pub. David C. Cook: Colorado Springs, Colorado

Wiseman, D. J. General editor. *Tyndale Old Testament Commentaries.* Intervarsity Press.

BIBLE VERSIONS

In addition to the *KJV* or *Authorised Version* of the Bible, the following versions or translations are cited, or were consulted by the author of this work.

CEV – *Contemporary English Version*; the American Bible Society, New York, NY; 1995.

ESV – *English Standard Version*; Crossway Bibles, a publishing ministry of Good News Publishers; Wheaton, Illinois; 2001.

GNB – *Good News Bible*; Second Edition, by the American Bible Society; New York, NY; 1992.

GW – *God's* Word; God's Word to the Nations Bible Society; Cleveland, Ohio; 1995.

JPS – *The JPS* Bible; the Jewish Publication Society; Philadelphia, PA; 1995.

ISV – *International Standard Version*, v. 1.2.2; The ISV Foundation, La Mirada, CA; 2001.

NET – *The Net Bible*; Biblical Studies Press; Richardson, Texas; 2006.

NIV – *New International Version*; Zondervan Bible Publishers, Grand Rapids, Michigan; 1978.

NJB – *New Jerusalem Bible*; Doubleday & Co. Inc; Garden City, New York; 1985

NRSV – *New Revised Standard Version*; the Division of Christian Education of the National Council of the Churches of Christ in the USA; 1989.

REB – *Revised English Bible with Apocrypha*; Oxford University Press; 1989.

YLT – *Young's Literal Translation*

www.ingramcontent.com/pod-product-compliance
Lightning Source LLC
Chambersburg PA
CBHW070533170426
43200CB00011B/2408